INKED-IN THOUGHTS

LEARNINGS FROM INTERACTIONS

BALWINDER

Copyright © Balwinder
All Rights Reserved.

This book has been published with all efforts taken to make the material error-free after the consent of the author. However, the author and the publisher do not assume and hereby disclaim any liability to any party for any loss, damage, or disruption caused by errors or omissions, whether such errors or omissions result from negligence, accident, or any other cause.

While every effort has been made to avoid any mistake or omission, this publication is being sold on the condition and understanding that neither the author nor the publishers or printers would be liable in any manner to any person by reason of any mistake or omission in this publication or for any action taken or omitted to be taken or advice rendered or accepted on the basis of this work. For any defect in printing or binding the publishers will be liable only to replace the defective copy by another copy of this work then available.

Dedicated in the loving memory of my father

S. Gurcharan Singh Bhatia

&

Blessings of my mother Mrs Darshan Kaur.

Contents

Contents

Contents

PREFACE

During my interactions with people across different geographies while spending more than 3 decades in service industry, i learned a lot about the behaviors, percpetions, practices and organizational cultures. Believe me despite all the IT inroads in our lives, human mind is still one major mystery still to be fully understood on how and why humans act, react and accept others' presence, interferences and dictats in personal and professional lives.

All that is written in this book is an honest reaction of mind towards happenings, chance encouters and interactions with my teams, business associates, leaders, customers and people from all walks of life.

ACKNOWLEDGEMENTS

Deeply indebted to my family for leaving enough room for me to scribble my thoughts and bring the same in the shape of this maiden book.

Big thanks to wife Sukhwinder "Dido", and lovely kids, daughter Arpit for being my first critic and editing my writings and son Archit for supporting my ideas.

I

Agree to disagree

Do agree to disagree. It is normal human behavior to align oneself with the majority opinion. The tendency to go along with the flow is always perceived as an easy option rather than voicing the dissent note. Even if we feel strongly about something we avoid being the first to raise our voice against it. In organizational meetings/discussions/seminars there is always an army of YES sayers.

But when people decide to remain mum on subjects with a fear of being singled out or proved wrong in the group, the genesis of ideation dies. Work culture should always encourage the spirit of agree to disagree. Don't look for blind endorsements but find the voice of dissent. Put the idea of counter views in healthy discussions to bring out the best. Even if the counter opinion is proved wrong, allowing it to come on the discussion table brings out the confidence in the team and endorses the feeling of being emotionally engaged. Creativity and ideation are the momentum of productivity and a healthy work environment. There is a need to agree to disagree in an endeavor to usher in transformative ideation.

II

April-appeasing

The much-hyped annual corporate ritual across industries is known as Appraisal month. Next day itself marks the Labor Day which means struggle is continuous.

Despite all challenges, predictable outcomes and critical reviews it remains an important event looked up to by the workforce.

For some it is up and raise.
    Some others are upped and razed.
    Some are showered with monetary blessings.
    Some others blessed get it all.
    For some it sums up the value they carry
    Some others have their own cake and cherry
    April pleases some worries many
    Work wonders or magic of destiny
    Like it or not, it is here to stay
    It weighs for you or directs you to a way.

III

Are you saleable?

Are you saleable? Were you there at the time and place when opportunity struck the doorbell? Are you vocal about your achievements and make a splash in your professional corridors? How many connections do you know who can pull a string for you at the time when your name makes round of the promotion's council or leadership search committee?

These and many more of similar nature questions make round of today's professionals who aspire to make his/her way up in the career ladder. Not very long ago the common advice for a young professional at the beginning of the career used to be "Do your job diligently and honestly "Rewards follow the one who follows the path of righteousness and doing the assigned job with dedication. But with the so-called modern-day management mantras which brought the HR again in focus of board room discussions, the very notion of eligible and fit criteria of "Future Leader" has undergone a change. The questions posed in the opening now come as desirables in a future leader.

It is okay to be nice. It is good to be honest and hardworking professional who knows his job well and carry on his team. What is the price of these attributes or what the value does these attributes carry for you? The simple answer would be that these attributes can be sufficient for making a monthly pay check but one must then live up leaving aside the aspirations to take the career ladder. The most desirable attribute is the salability. Your persona must carry the image of one who can beat the street always in achievements and in all weather conditions. So, one must learn to blow one's own trumpet.

Can you make a killing? Not to be understood as any illegal act or advice but the one who can learn the art of side stepping or taking steps on others shoulders. Learn to give the credit only wherever it is utmost required or cannot be avoided. Do make a moolah out of your teamwork and present it as finest leadership work. Learn to attract the praise and attention of those who matter.

Possessing these modern-day attributes is not a crime or any antisocial attribute. But it appears that professionals have now learned the art of rope walking so well that they know where the other end of rope is and who is handling the same in the boardroom. It is still nice to be a nice human being and one who feels the pain of sufferings of others but in professional life each step of the career ladder needs a price to be paid. This price is sometime sacrificing some of the age-old attributes of niceties and hardworking doing the job diligently. It asks for adding one new mantra or polishing the age-old attributes and placing them along with new professional attributes like being saleable.

Learn the art of selling oneself by showcasing what you possess and can do the best. " Jo dikhta hai wahi bikta hai" it is only the visible that gets counted.

IV

Art of accepting NO

How true and sustainable are the corporate relations? Perhaps even modern-day artificial intelligence will also fail to answer it correctly. The reason could be that all these are based on underlying objective of a commercial deal that has to satisfy the partners. As any analyst of human relation will put, the relations based on commercial objective are always prone to be on wavering track. Some analyst will term it as a test of loyalty which in modern times is a big "responsibility" word derived from the ancient times not in much favor in present day corporate world across the industries.

Are you under an obligation to be nice in your office? If you have come across such feeling, then you may not be alone to have such an experience. Majority of the supervisor and reportee relations are woven around the unwritten law of behaving nice. Decorum wise and as per basic HR practices, staff is expected to behave nicely with each other and ensure to follow manners and respect for the others. But this natural trait becomes a forced habit in many cases. You tend to say "Yes" even though unwillingly and that's what led to many personal help authors to write books like "The art of saying No".

The basic question is why we are obligated to be nice or saying yes in corporate relations. The obvious answer of employee employer relationship syndrome can take us through the times of evolution of corporate culture. Right from the ancient times labour or working class could hardly feel being heard or taking any sustainable stand because of weaker economic standings. The same scenario prevailed in the trading and newly set up industrial era wherein the will of owners fondly called "Seth" always prevailed. The policy of hire and fire at will, remained in corporate culture and still prevails as a management right. From the strict administrators donning Hitler like attributes to present day diplomatic tools of dealing with workforce, underlying principle continues..........................Keeping the workforce entangled in the race of being in good books of the people who matter. The ways and means of doing so are known all around. The superficial atmosphere of being good kills the free spirit of being true to oneself and ultimately being true to your organization.

When you know that displeasing the senior or boss is the risk you can't afford howsoever compelling your inner sole may be saying then it means that working conditions of the corporate are not conducive to keep workforce in good mental health. With all sort of transformations in industry, ways of doing the business and changing working scenarios in organisations, the biggest factor found wanting is inadequate transformation of leadership.

Owners to bosses and "the management" the whole hierarchy remains focused in managing rather than being creator or facilitator. We need to invest our efforts and thoughts in creating an organizational environment wherein thoughts and opinions have their natural flow without any danger or hindrance. Leaders are accepted when they learn to listen to the divergent opinions and come forward to make amends in larger interest of their organizations.

Managers or leaders in all types of industries, are often found mandated to go by single stream of "thoughts" coming from the top but in the process the machinery that gets the things happen on the ground starts feeling alienated. As a natural human desire of being attached to especially with the person or group that matters creates different work rules or just one rule of "Yes Sir" in the organization. In the present times of young working population opinions and thoughts from the ground are actually gaining ground in decision making at the top. The leaders are expected and well accepted too when they create an atmosphere of openness and let HR spirit flourish. To think different cannot be termed as being indifferent as it can often lead to uncharted ways of success.

Read somewhere a beautiful thought "There are people who make others happy wherever they go. There are also people who make others happy whenever they go". That sums up the thought of developing an art of accepting NO.

V

Be yourself

Advertisement lines are often taken as a means of commercial communication only. But if you pause for a minute, in today's high paced life, these lines sometimes tend to direct you to do some soul searching. It also leads to awakening or realizing the true purpose of living thus prompting to be yourself.

Just came across some lines from a famous tea brand which invoke the desire to be yourself as an individual without carrying the baggage of flashy titles or positions:

"Khud se milo" meet yourself
"Sukoon ka Riyaz" practice of tranquility
"Fursat wali chai" leisure time tea.

Going through these lines make us to realize the distance that has crept in ourselves and our identities.
Most of us tend to remain commercially engaged and wear

the material successes up on our sleeves. We try to know about ourselves from the perspective of others and lose our own individuality as a simple human being.

Try to be yourself sometimes and celebrate your own company. That's what even yoga, meditation or prayers mean by self-awakening.

Let's start making peace with ourselves to celebrate independence.

VI

Being contrarian

Every human being has an inbuilt desire of being liked or accepted. Many times, we tend to be part of the majority rather than being singled out. Howsoever we may be convinced within ourselves against the idea/proposal, we fail in mustering the courage to go against the tide. Why does it happen? Do we seek support from the group/crowd to back our point of view? Why do we seek validation from people? Who are those who dare to put forward their point of view knowing well it may not find favor with those proposing it? Answers to these questions and the psychology behind it led to this article.

The first and foremost reason behind why we aspire to be with group/leader rather being seen against is our basic human need of being liked and accepted. As Maslow figured out, it is part of our basic social need. Just have a look at the expanded modern world of our society in terms of social media and see how many photographs, selfies, quotes, posts, articles are being shared on all platforms. What do we look for by putting our lives up in the world of web for everyone to see, caressing our desire of being noticed and off course being liked?

Now the question comes why do we feel bound to say yes? It may be our internal lack of confidence or sense of our idea/objection being ruled out for acceptance. It has also its reasons ingrained in our upbringing. Do we encourage our kids to ask questions or just brush aside their queries terming as irrelevant? The younger generation better put as Gen Y is already brimming up with knowledge and have all forms of avenues available for their answers. But still, if raising a question or putting up individual point of view is encouraged at homes, we can have many more contrarians. The same logic applies to our workplaces. Do you feel encouraged to raise questions? How do the managers behave when someone from the team takes a contrarian view? According to HR experts, when the workers are encouraged to raise questions, the workplace has one of the basic criteria fulfilled for being called a healthy workplace.

A popular belief at workplace is to win over your teams to achieve organizational goals. Without taking a confronting stand, a suggestion would be to create a winning spirit among the members so that each individual aspires to taste the victory. Even if all team members' spirit does not get ignited with your efforts, still the game is sure to be won because the ignited members are able to create a positive and winning atmosphere at workplace.

What is being contrarian? In simple terms, the word means the one who opposes or rejects the popular opinion or current practice. Keep in mind that putting forward a contrarian view is not the same as confronting someone. As explained by Paul Krugman, "in its modern form, contrarianism presents an appearance of independent thought while failing to challenge, or actually reinforcing, the dominant orthodoxy of the political and media establishment."

Contrarianism does not mean being a villain or a negative character of a movie that is resented in the end. More so, it is not out of compulsion that one has to be contrarian. There has to be one, an independent thought and second, an alternative doable action plan which can justify the thought of a contrarian.

Conformists are those who conform unthinkingly to the usual practices or standards of a group or society. This in no way suggests that it is wrong being a conformist. Rather in societal set up it is appropriate and is required for smooth running of social life. But it is advantageous to have contrarians at workplace to give a challenge to existing practices. To have positive disruptions and create fresh thoughts/processes of workplace rules/productivity, contrarian thoughts often create new possibilities. The world-renowned contrarians such as Gandhi, Martin Luther King, Mohammad Ali and Steve Jobs have changed the world.

A quality contrarian leaders seem to possess is being an artful listener as it not only gives an excellent access to new ideas but also leads to careful evaluation of new information. Further contrarian thought also believes that it's always the great people, not great job descriptions that make organizations successful. The leaders who are forward-thinking and are not afraid of status-quo being challenged or their ideas being questioned inspire the teams to be contrarian and come out with disruptions.

The spoken words have magical impact on workforce as each human mind has the deepest desire of being addressed or spoken to. It helps in inspiring the teams and touching their emotional chord. Hierarchy rules of top-down approach may not find favor with contrarians. They know the meaning of getting the feedback at the ground.

Often organizational rules will require you to be firm. Contrarian thought suggests avoiding unnecessary humiliation of one who is already a defeated opponent. Being a supervisor or head of department, contrarian thought does suggest showing that you work for those who are working for you and believe in investing your time and energy in helping them succeed.

According to conformist thought, winning teams are foundations for success. But these are not coming as readymade out of the shelf product. Only robots are perfect conformists who can follow the rule of numbers to ensure your success at dashboards. Just taking a different approach may be called as contrarian. Start believing in creating the desire to succeed in teams and you may not even feel the need to say that your survival is dependent on your team's success. Creating an interest which attracts efforts of the workforce and encourages them to attempt is much more meaningful than simply handing over numbers to be achieved during a given time frame.

The similar approach is quite actively used in investor communities around the world. Contrarian investing is an investment strategy that is characterized by purchasing and selling in contrast to the prevailing sentiment of the time. On being contrarian or follower of contrarian theory of investment, an investor Ben Graham said "You are neither right nor wrong because the crowd disagrees with you. You are right because your data and reasoning are right."

Being contrarian requires to be a keen observer of the world around you with continuously figuring out the 'how' and 'why' of basic principles. This thought process makes us move forward and help the world in coming up with innovations and achieving progress. Positive disruptions happening around us today are the possibilities created by contrarian minds around us.

VII

Belongingness

"Belongingness is the human emotional need to be accepted member of a group. The need to belong is the need to give, and receive attention to, and from, others." ....so defines the Wikipedia.

Maslow's pyramid of hierarchical needs has often been taken as a base to study the human needs and also a tool by HR professionals to put in place the strategies to form HR policies. This scenario with the passage of time as any other belief has undergone a change. Evolution of job hopping, movement across verticals, industries and even continents have forced the HR thinkers to reassess the Maslow and pyramid of human needs in present day context.

The present-day organizations are now reckoning a major force called "Millennials" a young and vibrant work force not only as employees but also as a major constituent of target population for sales. Digital age and IT are now redefining the way we approach structure of needs and base our strategies. Social media and ease of connectivity has also led to other challenges in defining and projecting the "Place to Work With".

With this scenario, the HR thinkers had a relook on Maslow and observed that present human force look upon social connections or more broadly put belongingness as the one of the main driving forces of human behavior. Dr. Pamela Rutledge, an expert on social media issues observed in an article that Maslow misses the role of social connection in his grid of needs.

Our workforce now expects this to be the feature of workplace after having been grown in inter-connected world as sense of belongingness makes them feel secure and safe. This may have led to birth of idea called Radical Management which has defined the way of managing the organizations in today's scenario. As defined by Steve Denning author of Leader's guide to Radical management "Radical Management is a way of managing organizations that generates at the same time high productivity, continuous innovation, deep job satisfaction and customer delight"

Having a deep review of definition, one can make out that it well defines the vision, mission and strategic stand of organizations and the base of other organizational decisions including those related HR, Finance, Sales and future positioning.

Taking a clue further from Radical Management in our present subject context, one of the principles of this theory says that managers now have to change the way of conducting themselves. There has to be a shift from mere control activity of managers to more dynamic role of "Enablers". As is the expectation of today's workforce, this changed approach "will help in liberating the energies and talents of those doing the work and remove impediments that are getting in the way of work."

The theory further makes a point emphasizing that this shift also deals with workforce and end users to be dealt as "independent, thinking, feeling human beings." As is the mindset of workforce being well rooted in connected world, complexities are no more hurdles for them. Rather these are perceived as opportunities and an encouragement in themselves to challenge these complex situations/scenarios and emerge winners.

Taking a clue on similar lines of Maslow and assessing present day human capital, Sanjay Sathe of Rise Smart has expressed for Human Capital that key to managing the same is to treat them as true investment. Creating of an environment enabling both the employee and organization to reap rewards and extending employee engagement beyond the recruitment are important for management of human capital. Recognition, review and learning processes should actually engage with employees and should not be just perceived as mere token by workforce.

For today's workforce, belongingness and meaningful engagement are playing much more important role in assessing their needs. Our ways of assessment, measurement of goals achievement, rewards and recognition programs and fast track routes have to be built around these needs. One measurement does not fit all. As said by Deb Cupp of SAP, "Instead of just focusing on top performers, think of everyone as talent". This is required to dispel the beliefs that organizations reward and recognize only the "cash cows" but is influenced and moved by others too who also ran.

Mountains can be moved if efforts are directed with harnessing the exact needs which may not fall in hierarchal order, that fuels the sense of ownership, reward of efforts and a sense of belonging to the group that feels elated over success ....of individual efforts in making organizational success. Let the vision be woven by engaging all to ensure that all have a pie to share of organizational success in terms of their career advancement, recognition and a pride to belong.

VIII

BHK-O

In some quite distant past, a Hindi film song used to be very popular with words "ik bangla bane nyara, jis mein rahe kumbha saara" meaning let's have a bungalow like such wherein whole family may stay together". See how the tide of time has taken a turn that movement of joint families splitting into nuclear units is turning its tail. Present times, may be due to economic and/or safety compulsions, have made this happen. In WFH scenario, people are moving to family homes and are staying together.

Now our housing industry needs to change by coming up with concept of BHK O (office) offerings to suit the requirements. It's also required to address the concern of family members that WFH is encroaching upon their space and freedom. Stanford Economist Nicholas Bloom is sounding alarm on continued WFH as it impacts children, space, privacy and choice. Risk of privacy invasion in zoom meetings acts as continued pressure on minds.

So, need is to redesign our spaces to have Work, Family and all in one place called home and go for BHK with O.

Maybe we see in tomorrow's newspaper: Wanted: 2/3 BHKO with 24 hours Wi-fi.

IX

Captive minds

We often come across increasing and unabated load of information, instructions and invigilation in personal and professional lives. These uncontrolled attacks are piercing into our thought process. These are now even controlling our thoughts and influencing the decision-making. We are becoming conscious enslaves to the world around us. One of the articles by Alternative Thinking on Psychology and Mental Health, puts it as conditioned consciousness or enslaved consciousness. The artificial or manmade world around us is compelling to do whatever the conditioning, mechanical impulses of thinking want it do.

Our craving to remain a tech-savvy locks our thinking into gadgets and AI driven processes. Needs are processed/ programmed by profit-hungry businesses to be embedded in our lives. Weak and emotional areas are commercialized to lay out the sales pitch. Impulsive consumption becomes growth agent.

Informational and instructional flow creates fear of

missing out and keeps us trapped in 4-6 inches window of modern Gurukul. No doubt this system creates more followers than thinkers or leaders. Dissent is discouraged by design. Captive minds remain in delusion that we are in pursuit of fulfilment of our needs and goals. However, the invisible coercion and cajoling of commercial world keeps us following the designed needs and remain trapped in vicious circle of fulfilment thereof.

We are rapidly losing on the discoverers and inventors as free access to everything which is being channelized premeditated way is destroying the curiosity to think and ask. No one else to blame but ourselves. Look out for the needs and purposes being served by them before succumbing to conditioned consciousness. Encourage the curiosity and motivate the free questioning.

Curiosity opens doors in pursuit of knowledge and freedom of thoughts. Best medicine for good mental health is free minds where consciousness is not enslaved to outside world.

X

The Change Time

Change is the only constant. Change brings opportunities. Change sustains life. All these characteristics of change emphasize the importance of change in our lives. Where is the life constant? Time is always on the move. One has to be on the move (forward) always to survive. Even in Jungle life (animal kingdom) survival is possible only if you sustain the changes.

Change in itself is a double-sided coin. On one side is Opportunity and the other side is Threat. They both go hand in hand.

Opportunities if you:

Accept the change

Carry the change

Be the change

Not go for changing the change.

It poses threats also as it brings:

Disruption

Relook at what may not be wrong but can be improved

Rewriting the rule book to get along the change.

We all get excited and worried simultaneously on change. Even if the change is happening at the extreme end of your work chain or life system still it creates some ripples in still water of our thought processes. The first impact is announcement of the change itself. How do you arrive or make your first announcement on the need of change?

At any stage of an organizational life change brings about different impact. Like the childhood or formation stage, teens or getting the act together and maturity or adulthood of the organization life. Need of change is also seen from different perspective by internal stakeholders and by the change agent itself. There is a need to change the systems/processes to achieve the revised goals or due to revised rules of the game. Change is being effected since existing systems are at fault or failed to bring about the desired results. Both the statements emphasize on change but one conveys the need with positivity and other by equating the existing structure/systems to a failure.

Now something to dwell upon the change agent itself. Any new introduction of people, process and policies or all put together can be a change agent. People or processes change bring out the anxious reactions on the way it is rolled out. No one can deny the fact that any change can never be without the expected "Outcomes" which may be betterment of timings, process quality, and achievement of numbers (budget/growth) or meeting out interests of the stakeholders in any organization. These "Outcomes" are part and parcel of the promised change as these in themselves carry the genesis of the change.

If change is being carried out for the better it no way conveys the meaning that whatsoever has happened till the arrival of "Change" was wrong, outdated or a failure. Rather it should be seen as set of new means to look at our ways of attempting/accepting the things and carrying them to logical end in better way to have improved results.

Change can be pain or pleasure the way same is implemented. First the message of change itself has to be released or conveyed to the target audience in such a manner that it is understood in the same meaning as it is intended by the Change Agent. Next in line of action should be to create some more change agents who in themselves are convinced about the change and are ready to take it to hierarchal layers as "owner of the process" rather than spreading the change message "as told to us".

Change consultant William Bridges' model clarifies that how people adjust to change. The model features three stages: a stage for *letting go*, a stage of *uncertainty and confusion* and a stage for *acceptance*.

During the change times, another important angle requires attention is human side of the change. Is it being duly addressed by Change Approach? As has been often observed that change/transformation ushers in an era where there is an expectation from the cadre to step up, improve the capabilities and learn new skills. This causes great amount of uncertainty and resistance among the resources. Skillful engagement of the resources and getting along the target audience with a clear/defined need of change as "New Mission Statement" can drive the organization in such times.

A success of Change will be measured in results which are produced by resources of an organization. If Change Initiative is better understood and adopted by the resources it can make Change Times a smooth exercise as ultimately it is the resource that undergoes changed ways of doing the jobs.

As defined by Jeffery Hiatt the founder of ADKAR model of change management, to make any Change a success, resources/people of organization have to go through the following stages:

Awareness of the need for a change.

Desire to support the change.

Knowledge of how to change.

Ability to demonstrate skills and behaviors. (Coaching, feedback).

Reinforcement to make the change stick. (Open communication, rewards).

Quoting Peter Senge to conclude Change Times..."
People don't resist change. They resist being changed."

XI
Change- a process

Repetitive processes or people bring complacency. It grows in human behavior and discourages experimentation. Humans are not immortal in nature, but our attitudes often show the opposite. Illusion of permanence of power, position and patrimony bring unnecessary hegemony.

Continuous oppression sows the seeds of change. Ignoring the dissent and being indifferent to the locals creates a movement that empowers change.

Mass and resources are learning to see through the changes mandated by leaders which are useful to class not the mass. A swarm of flashy ideas may not sell well to those who struggle around their daily and basic needs. Processes and policies which fail to ameliorate the living standards of people on the ground remain a hollow promise of empowerment.

Pragmatic thought process, acceptability of challenge and enthusiasm to make society a healthier planet bring about desirable sustainable changes. Countries and organizations that are interested in leaving the families of prosperous citizens and workers as a payback to society, rather than having the leaders focusing on enriching their clans, have hope for continuous change and sustainable growth.

Change is only permanent factor in evolution of the mankind.

XII

Corporate Symphony

Melody is known as collection of musical notes grouped together as single entity. Harmony in turn is a musical accord complimenting melody grouping individual musical voices. Harmonious combination of melodies creates Symphony.

An ensemble of artists performing together a musical piece, creates a symphony. One artist playing an instrument who is joined by other artist's playing different instruments. Rendition happens in a flow while other artists keep on joining playing their part in sync. No one tries to outplay the other or tries hogging the limelight even after joining last. It becomes an artwork of melody where every tone and tune are seen complimenting the other instrument.

Musical journey of Symphony resembles a lot with working

culture in organizations. Substituting melody with resources/people explains corporate story. Acceptance/adoption/appreciation of existing melodies motivate improvisations and lead to harmonious emergence for the new tunes.

•

Melodies remain ingrained in the system. Conductor create harmony by grouping individual musical voices (resources) together and by playing on their strengths. Corporate actions have to just tune in the consonant notes for achieving harmonious melody which brings in a Corporate Symphony.

XIII

Has your Cheese been moved?

While recollecting reading of a book called "Who moved my cheese "and evaluating the same in world around us, led to writing of this post.

It is a fact for individuals as well for organizations that any stream of earnings, workings or processes cannot be taken for lasting forever without any disruption. Especially in today's world where intelligence has moved to Artificial Intelligence and human behaviors are being imbibed in Robots to do routine jobs, changes or disruptions whichever way you may like to describe are here to stay and guide our future. Taking it to the subject, the assumptions or understandings of earlier times are now being put to challenges. Experimentation is the key world and it is delivering lot of new kids on the block that are pushing the traditional boundaries of ways and means of conducting yourself and doing the business.

Now let's take this statement to commercial world and see how the disruptions are actually taking away cheese of business that is stream of revenues of someone and creating new "cheese" for others.

With the announcement of issuing license of new banks (Payment and Small), the scenario in existing players was assessed in both ways. Will the new players eat away the CASA or lure the target generation with new IT enabled offerings. Will staff poaching will add to existing worries of HR or make their task easier in getting rid of extra flap in the wake of controlling costs? That led to moving of cheese (business opportunities) of someone. Others view it as a positive disruption and started for upcoming territories to look for "cheese" there to ensure that new ground can compensate by yielding the required numbers that have come under threat.

The other industry, telecom witnessed arrival of giant player with the kind of offerings that put the ground rules upside down. Mere announcement itself moved the tonnes of "cheese" from the financial stores of established players of industry. Those who can have the wherewithal to stand up to competition take it as a positive challenge to showcase the strength they have built up in their customer base and networks. They initiated moves to find out other niche areas to make up for part of potential hit to business thereby ensuring that their piece of "cheese" is not compromised.

The next case in Indian corporate world is one that worked well on evoking patriotism in consumerism and led to a challenge to MNCs. Selling Ayurveda products in India is nothing new but the way opportunity (Maggi crash) got encashed and led to arrival of Indianness in every household put the bigger players in a sense of disbelief as to how an indigenous challenge has taken away their "cheese" in front of their eyes. Just by invoking the spirit of being Indian and buying Indian made its presence felt and made the consumers to taste the new cheese with a salt of patriotism. The MNCs who were having unwritten monopoly on these markets realized that "cheese" in any market cannot be taken for granted. Newer ways and means are must to not only protect your share but to look for fresh grounds to get new "cheese".

Another case of Indian corporate relating to not-too-distant past relates to our "Hamara Scooter" a well-known brand of two wheelers. With continued success over decades on similar products, the company starts having diminishing law of return of corporate success or "kick" out of the same model of success. There arrives a new challenger with requirements of modern or today's generation and vroom goes of its model of success. The gearless and swanky two-wheeler just took away the whole pie in such a fashion that it led to believe for existing player that no more "cheese" can be extracted now from given product line. But as the things turned out that market went gaga over new variety and accepted the change with open arms.

Satisfaction of end users or consumers whatsoever we may call is to be watched carefully and constantly. The only thing constant in the world is change. So, before you come under threat of your cheese being moved, assess the sustainability and scalability of your product line over the time horizon. Evaluate it with ever changing tastes and preferences of consumer and keep on offering different tastes/versions. Market remains the same for all new and old players but only thing differentiate is the product offering that can alter the scenario. Many at times it is the product and its marketing that defines the future tastes of the consumers.

Another important factor to ensure safety and continuity of existing "cheese" is to always look forward to feedback...honest feedback. Encourage the critical review from the ground and try to mould and evaluate the same for future planning. Don't let someone to move your cheese by continuously improving upon the processes and strategies to not only safeguard existing resource and revenues but to find the new one to cope up with uncertain times.

Here are some of the important lessons of widely read book "Who moved my cheese" by Spencer Johnson.

"Noticing small changes early helps, you adapt to the bigger changes that are to come"

"Old belief does not lead you to new cheese"

"Smell the cheese often so you know when it is getting old."

"Being in the uncomfortable zone is much better than staying in the cheese-less situation."

So be on guard and look for newer ways to get more and different versions of "Cheese".

XIV

Crisis of confidence

The crisis of confidence is often discussed in terms of an individual problem as well as an institutional or organizational issue. At individual level, a famous Bollywood personality running campaign on highlighting this problem says "dobara poochna" ask again. This short but hard-hitting response on crisis of confidence or depression in individual lives sums up what often lacks in our approach towards those facing this problem. There is need to probe further and go beyond what meets the eye.

In commercial organizations, the vulnerability to risk can never be ignored. For commercial crisis, in one of the studies published on the same subject, it has been defined as an event with low probability which causes extensive damage and social disruptions involving a variety of stakeholders. Being a part of commercial world, let's analyze this issue in commercial organizations. Lots of case studies have been published citing this problem faced by organizations across the world. Expert views have been shared on the approaches the organizations took and how they battled the same and came out of it. GM, BMW, Johnson

& Johnson, Pepsi, Nestle India (Maggi), Volkswagen emissions and financial industry (Banks/NBFCs) in India are some of the industry players who have faced the said crisis. Many at times it has turned out to be a crisis of communication, clarity on roles, cohesive approach to address the concerns.

Without going into the reasons of crisis or what led to this crisis, it is important to have a look on how these crises have been handled. First and foremost, two lines of action are seen running parallel. One is the management thought and other is palpable reaction process of internal stakeholders to information onslaught from external and internal sources. Some of the corporates quoted above have faced this problem in pre-social networking era and have thus had impact as per reach of the print and visual media. However, for others, social media put the crisis on a wider canvas and accordingly the process to handle the crisis changed considerably. Reason for emphasizing on use of social media can be best described in one of the famous quotes that say "a lie travels around the globe while the truth is putting on its shoes". Even though all that comes on social media cannot be put as total lie or truth, it definitely impacts the mindset of consumers.

On management thought processes and ways put to use to defuse the crisis, often we find the refusal to accept what has happened. However, some of the organizations learned to play safe and handled the crises with first accepting what has happened. The next in line of action is handling of information onslaught, which would have caused considerable clouds of doubts in the mind of stake holders. This has been often seen with considerable increase in competitor's activities within the industry to prove the point. On having a look at the various approaches adopted by different corporates in crisis of confidence, it has been seen that management's first action in arresting the damage is always to address the external stakeholders. Although approach may be different but underlying thought remains the same to assuage the feelings of target consumer base and off-course to simultaneously address the regulator concerns. Remedial measures to put corrective processes in place are follow up action of management thought process.

The next parallel line of action which has proved to be useful whenever implemented across organizations is role of internal stakeholders. In the wake of free flow of information through various channels including social media, often internal stakeholders are left to draw their own conclusions. Given the approachability of such resources and their relationships across the customer base of the organization, managing the crisis proves to be much effective through the services of these resources. Ground force or field force has been found delivering the confidence in a much better way to end users as an effective spokesperson of his/her targeted audience.

Media is another important factor which decides how well an organization is equipped to face the crisis and able to come out of it. As discussed in the opening, the same happens in individual situations, your social circle impacts the way you handle the crisis and how you come out of it. Given the autonomy and authority, media onslaught is inevitable. The role of spokesperson, quality and content of messages for the public are equally important to have the desired impact to soothe the sentiments.

Media meetings, campaigns on the organizational strengths and brief on being with consumers in difficult times of crisis and sharing the way forward has helped the organizations in making a positive move for coming out of the crisis.

As explained by Pauchant and Mitro in their Onion model of crisis management, changes happen only at the outer layer of the onion i.e., structures and plans of organization but these are actually required to happen at the inner layer of the onion i.e., individuals' subjective beliefs and assumptions. For effective management or preparedness to handle crisis, focus of managers has to be on culture and individual beliefs and assumptions which form core of organizational structure.

Effective leveraging of Management, Men (resource base), Methods (processes) and Media by organizations is the key to keep them prepared for such eventuality and effectively deal with it.

XV

Daag achhe hain (Stains are good)

A famous tagline of one of the leading washing powder manufacturers in India. It proclaims to take care of your worries of stained clothes. It is further packaged with the emotional pitch of children's innocent game play. Even celebrities are shown smiling on having tumbled the dishes on designer dresses.

Just go beyond these emotional pitches to find out as to whose interests are being served? By asking you to take time off from your worries of stained clothes you are being turned into an impulsive buyer for the company products.

This is a smart corporate play colored with emotional pitch. In most of such corporate pitches on products, processes and people we tend to be oblivion of whose interests are being served in the end.

In a similar way these days, corporate are found self-justifying by saying attrition is good. Rationale being offered is that people are now more open to experiment and discover. On the flip side it is a revenue stream for recruitment agencies and saving big bucks for corporate on mandated long service entitlements.

Concept of selling of stains concerns by corporate across industries is serving just one directional interest. This is major disengagement factor in the workforce from millennial to Generation-Z. It fails to strike a chord with the end user for process/product/program which is conceptualized in corner rooms without factoring in the interests of end users.

What's in for me? It may sound selfish but it makes valid engagement factor for the users in believing that though stains are not good but there is a facilitation being offered to address the concerns genuinely. Goals which are mutually beneficial, enriching and compliment interests of stakeholders/corporate and consumers create lasting impressions without stains in relationships.

XVI

Denial mode of Leadership

Often, we have come across the fact that during passing on operational orders in military establishments the final word to conclude the dialogue is " Koi Shaq"....any doubt (on implementation)? The reply as expected is always "No Sir". Then it is left to the unit/platoon head to do or die in the operation. But he is free to escalate the ground realities like need for cover fire, back up of ammunitions or further enforcement to the higher ups. The need continues to change as per ground information and requirements thereof. Leaders are bound to take those inputs for providing the help to make the mission successful.

Change the scene to corporate world. It's not only that we find the case of not knowing the realities but more often we are in situations where there is refusal to accept the realities. The hierarchy of leadership often tends to block or refuse to accept the "not so good" news coming from the operational fronts and will hesitate to present the same to top leadership. The simplest reason could be that it may be seen by top managements as their (middle management's) incompetence to handle the crisis or uncomfortable news. So, the middle managers continue to make themselves and those on top believe that all is well. Does it help in ignoring the problem or refusal to accept that there are issues to be addressed? Why do leaders' resort to denial?

In an article published by HBR, the psychological concept Denial has been defined as a "mechanism that helps a person avoid a potentially distressing truth. It can also be looked at as a form of avoidance, which is another psychological term which indicates that a person is doing all they can to not deal with a given situation". This form of avoidance more particularly described as "denial" in leadership behavior impacts the working atmosphere. Teams who look up to the leaders to address the issues or through proper escalation to top management in the cases involving policy matters, start losing hope in view of denial by immediate leaders. It also leads to unhealthy behavior and toxic working atmosphere. It's like a scenario of leadership fooling them into thinking that they have control over a situation when in reality they don't.

It is often seen that leadership in denial mode tends to put the entire blame on "them" i.e., the entire team. They prefer to be surrounded by like-minded people who ascribe to their opinions. That helps them in validating their opinions and protecting their ego when they put up a false stand in front of the seniors leading them to believe that nothing needs to be addressed. In scenarios like these, anyone offering a different perspective or asking uncomfortable questions might help accept the problem and can also prompt people to search for a solution. But in scenarios wherein the leadership is in denial, those offering different perspectives are seen as "unwelcome" guests or getting unnecessarily perturbed by "minor" turbulence.

It is often cited in management history that denial of leadership has played a major role in the decline of companies. One of the most often quoted examples is that of US Automobile Industry. It refused to recognize the changes that were occurring in consumer demand/tastes and refused to take appropriate action at the right time. Similar instances are quoted for Kodak, Music industry (LP records), PC industry and traditional two wheelers (scooters) of Indian market. They also showed signs of ignoring external changes like disruptive technological innovations and often overestimated their corporate capabilities. The similar trend of decline can also be observed in political organizations/groups wherein the information flow from bottom to top is censored.

Denial can not only be blamed on leadership of an organization but also on the atmosphere within the organization. It also reflects in organizations facing crisis of confidence. If raising concerns or asking of questions is encouraged, it is the sign of a positive organizational atmosphere that motivates people to speak up. Escalation of uncomfortable scenarios should not be seen as an attempt to hurt the ego or sacrifice one's position in the eyes of top management. Free flow of thoughts and ideas is like oxygen in any organization. Denial in leadership at any stage of hierarchy can act like a gas chamber bringing death to innovative minds. It's like veins stopping the flow of much needed blood and oxygen to the brain. Free flow of information, without being censored from bottom to top can encourage the leaderships in all hierarchy levels to strive for the best for an organization. There is a need to ensure and demonstrate the fact that the leadership is willing to accept and listen to uncomfortable news in positive way and has the strength to work on the same.

Organizations should encourage the leadership to move from denial mode to deliberation tables and exhibit the will to resolve by accepting that working organizations do have some "uncomfortable" moments. By accepting and working on them, one can move the organizational story forward.

XVII

Disruptive innovations and Information Age

As defined by Clayton Christensen the disruptive innovation is a process by which product or services take root initially in simple applications at the bottom of the market and then relentlessly moves up market and then displacing established competitors.

Now look at Information Age which has the advent of Digital revolution talked and discussed as parallel of Agriculture and Industrial revolution as one of the major factors of transformation in the way we do business, think about business and assess the needs of business.

Both the above changes that have happened in the present times are having major impact on the commerce and economy of a nation. There is a race amongst nations to not only adapt to these changes and acclimatize to them but also to outrun others in declaring their processes smart, cities smart and citizens smart. These are also being seen as a way to cut too old and lethargic age-old processes and most debated, and end to corruption. This is also seen as a direct connect between the major target population of the country- the tech savvy young generation. Ease of doing and expanded reach with no geographical boundaries having whole world as one market is the visual that these changes are bringing in our lives. The market or shopping sites of the world have been squeezed into 4-5 inches of our mobile screens. App driven is the mantra of modern innovations that are happening daily and redefining the way we look at our basic needs and the ways to fulfil them.

All these new age innovations are about to bring a paradigm shift in our lives. These are having major impact on how the goods and services are processed and the way needs of consumers are being assessed processed and impacted through Disruptive innovations, Digital revolutions and last but not the least Big Data. Internet of Things (IOT) is another reality soon going to descend on our lives.

All these revolutions and changes are being perceived from process angles. But let's have a look at the same from the angle of delivery. The channel through which these are getting delivered or the set-up of any organization which is adopting these new innovations/changes. Are all the parties of a workplace wherever these processes are being integrated are clear about what, why and how about these changes? The human workforce has to be clear about the factors like how new innovation or processes are going to work. As every change is a challenge in itself the organizations need to take pain in explaining the changes which are required to be made in the existing processes to make way for new systems/processes to be adopted. And the most important is sharing the vision of the management in explaining what the new processes/innovations/changes are expected to deliver to the business.

Wherever in organizations these factors are left to be self-explained or implemented to be with the change, often we find the resistance to change and half-hearted attempt in accepting the same. This results in confusion in understanding the processes and fall in productivity. So, from delivery point of view the manpower which is there to face the end user and deliver on the new tech driven processes has to be trained or retrained on skills required. There is absolute need to devise suitable behavioral trainings to change the mindset for new age innovations and technologies. With reduced on the floor processing and greater interaction points with customers, manpower needs to understand the ways of processing that take place at the back-end. The front force that becomes touch point in brick-and-mortar structure of delivery points and staff at customer care centres need to be made mentally agile and technically awake to the processes/innovations adopted by organization and the ways how it has impacted the needs assessments of consumers.

So, at management level there is greater need to re-emphasize the vision with human resources and this subject needs to be revisited as many times as the new processes come to the fore. The more the human resource is made to share the vision, the way its achievement and living up to it is being perceived in ongoing tech revolutions, disruptive innovations posing challenges to the ways of doing business, they can deliver in much more productive manner. Let there be discussions on how, why and for whom these changes are being brought and in what ways these changes can impact positively or otherwise the lives of human resource of an organization. Let these staff be shown light at the end of tunnel of changes, the light that can bring about more for organization and human resources as well, no one will say No to walk down that lane. Change is law of nature and is inevitable and can bring about opportunities if worked together. As Maslow said, all humans are motivated by needs-may be in different orders of satisfaction but sense of being a part of success still holds good for all.

XVIII

Dissent

Consensus is not always a universal positive. Especially in commercial organizations wherein it translates to absence or suppression of voice of dissent. Top down led project or change is often greeted with stoic silence signifying dearth of opinion diversity. Leadership development experts term it as a process loss. It creates "command" of what to do but there is no or insufficient "want" to do. There is an absence of ownership of opinions as participation in decision making is either just a formality or "sleepers" just go along with what the majority say and endorse the decision.

The organization wherein participation is well represented by diverse opinion holders there is a freedom that encourages to agree to disagree with respect. People own up the change/tasks and deliver better. Voices if allowed to be heard especially those sounding a different note can result in a new melody.

It is important to create an atmosphere for people to open-up a note of dissent or for them to dare to be different. Participation with diversity of opinions results in better informed decisions and well-motivated "wants" to do.

XIX

Downfall: the case against Boeing-story

Corporate credibility, culture, competitive strength and compliance stature; all these superlatives of corporate world have been duly put to test in the aforementioned documentary which so precisely traced the skeletons from Boeing's closet and grounded the hyped-up standards. Undisputed leader of aviation industry went through tough times created by their own deeds and greed.

It beautifully explained the culture of convenience, merger of like-minded goals and never-ending desire of winning at any cost. Lower the costs at any cost and go for profits to any length.

Under unwritten oath, investors with deep pockets influence CEOs to ensure that increasing their wealth remains the corporate mantra. Discard old, lengthy and resource consuming processes for fast, easy to use, and light on corporate pocket operations/products.

Voice of dissent is discouraged, ignored and finally side stepped as an obstacle to efficiency and profitability. Stock markets become barometer of success of corporates and its key leaders running the show.

This story is often found running with almost the same script in many corporates around the world. Nice story that warrants many to see through the corporate methods carefully and examine if the same script is casting you aside.

XX

Evaluation

To appraise is to set a value or estimate worth. Humans generate numbers and numbers evaluate humans.

Many sectors have followed GE's famous forced ranking system of rewarding the top, accommodating the medium, and letting go of the bottom, which was first implemented in 1980. Experts discovered flaws such as resources being held accountable for previous performance instead of focusing on enhancing future performance. Its outcome has become predictable, and the practice has grown monotonous for both the resources and supervisors. It is failing to achieve the primary goal of motivation and engagement.

Various approaches have been used to position appraisal as a holistic evaluation that goes beyond numbers. Wal-Mart's Management by Objectives focuses on joint identification planning and communication of goals.

RBS and G4S' 360 Degree approach covers entire spectrum of touch points of a resource and feedback therefrom.

Microsoft and Philips' Assessment Centre Method examines competencies and exhaustive feedback in depth.

Behavioral Anchored Rating Scale rates workplace behavior against set standards.

P&G's Psychological Appraisal consists of psychological sessions used to determine interpersonal effectiveness and unearth hidden potentials.

HR cost accounting by startups makes cost benefit analysis of a resource. Revenue streams are weighed against the cost of retention.

Transactional paradigm of evaluation and pay rewards is changing. It is also necessary to assess effectiveness, empathy, ethical behavior and engagement levels.

Which one do you think is more effective?

XXI

Employee experience to Customer Experience

A commercial organization will always be on the lookout for ways to increase its share into customers' wallet. Homogeneous products with heterogeneous packaging are placed on the shelves. Big brand ad campaigns and celebrity endorsements are rolled out. Perfect recipe of product success is rolled out. This process invariably hinges on the involvement of delivery chain which has to ultimately conclude the product journey. Journey of the product pass through important phase called employee experience EX. This leg has direct correlation with end objective of product or service called Customer Experience CX. The importance of CX has led to increased relevance of CXOs in organizations who oversee product journey in all stages and ensures it reaches with all its flavors intact to the end user.

Are we missing on employee experience journey that correlates to better customer experience and translates to sales? To some extent answer is yes. Organizations invest heavily on products, processes and packaging thereof to stay relevant in the market. However, the EX that has huge impact on the moment of delivery of services/product called transaction is less thought about. The in-house brand ambassadors of the products/services are seen as mere delivery agents not the sale makers. Reason is lack of investment in EX the employee experience journey in organization. Since it deals with humans, all its processes i.e., emotions, anxiety, expectations and engagement levels cannot be automated or controlled through AI. Sustainable and successful CX depends upon level of EX in organization.

The impact of EX is being looked upon not only by organizations but by consumers of today also equally evaluate the product by its social relevance index or human value index. Consumers now look out for products proving humanitarian values which get showcased by satisfied employees. Many famous beauty product lines and clothing brands lost the favor of millennials because these corporate were seen as adopting discriminatory practices in dealing with workforce. Better EX is outcome of improved investment in employee's personal and professional development. As per human science experts, EX moves on TEA i.e., trust, empathy and attention. It helps translating organizational goals into reality as customer is serviced with pride, confidence and smile. Having engaged employees creates sustainable CX meeting out the ultimate objective of organizations in better revenues.

Customer centric product/service approach is often discussed and planned out by organizations. Having employee centric work culture is also now becoming the topic in board rooms planning to ensure richness of CX. High level of EX also helps employees in setting and achieving goals without being micro managed, learn, grow and thrive in the workplace. Corporate like Asby, SAP, HP and Cheesecake factory tasted success wherein rejuvenated employee experience led to refreshing customer experience and in turn resulted in customers' increased loyalty.

Success of commercial organizations is sustained through not only varied product line but also well invested and engaged employees.

XXII

Fault in the stars

The oft quoted statement in our lives when things do not happen the way we wish them to happen. Just examining the said statement in context of one of the movies with similar title called "Fault in Our Stars" gives another context to weigh our hardships. Astrology, stars and Horoscopes play an important role in our day to day lives wherever and whenever these are consulted with and acted upon. The correlation in the said statement and theme of the movie throws a light on our behaviors when we are struggling. The said struggle could be to achieve more, compete for success or overcome our disabilities or sufferings like chronic illness. On the similar sidelines we also tend to hear about the statement that hardships bring out the best in you.

Some of the often-repeated quotes from the movie:

"You don't get to choose if you get hurt in this world......
but you do have some say in who hurts you."

"The marks humans leave are too often scars".

"The world is not a wish-granting factory".

"Grief does not change you. It reveals you".

The above quotes although taken from the film dialogues but these speak about us and our way of taking on the struggle, obstacles, disabilities and challenges. These challenges could be of nature or man-made. Going through the quotes make you believe that challenges are always there to test our strengths and our abilities to overcome. It offers no solution by looking for fault in the stars. All have to endure the share of their challenges.

Extending the above learning to professional challenges and hurdles one has to go through which are more than often man-made, you tend to draw a different perspective. All the above quotes reflect beautifully in our professional lives and the way organizations live up to. Right from the first quote on being hurt to leaving the scars, these experiences are most common in professional behaviors. And who can dispute the fact on "world" or your organization is not a wish-granting factory.

Why one is made to relive the statement of fault in the stars? This phrase comes up on going through the phase where in one- upmanship is often found practiced. People are judged or assessed based on competitive strengths rather than individual contribution. Competitive strength although is a positive trait requires in leaderships or aspiring leaders but its usage is found in being smarter than other. The end results or numbers on assessment matters more than means adopted to reach the goals.

So, it's not fault in the stars of one who is adjudged on the lower rankings vis a vis one who got the top billings, it is the positioning of stars who topped the charts. The positioning is not one that is subject matter of astronomy but one that is fixed in organizational galaxy. The closeness to power star and your revolution that is movement around power star strengthens the positioning.

XXIII

Ferrari in our lives

Ferrari cars are generally seen as cars meant for racing. But just have a look at the style statement it makes in society as a symbol of speed, luxury and wealth. These are the attributes of the brand called Ferrari. Besides being an established brand in motor sports it is also acts as success brand of commercial world being run on speed adding layers of luxury in the store of wealth.

If we look at the qualities of speed it gives adrenaline rush to the driver. Putting a foot on gas pedal of Ferrari itself make the romance of speed rush in the veins. Moreover, the kind of media positioning it gets with motor racing; it becomes synonymous with high pitch sound of speed. In such races, definitely it's a race to win over the others with your speed and moves but it is also a chance to establish the supremacy of your brand which is being driven. So, the takeaway is that not only running the race that matters but the vehicle i.e., path of process chosen to run the race also matters.

Ferrari is known around the world as symbol of speed, luxury and wealth. If we correlate these attributes in commercial world success, these are the same factors which drive the passion. Success in commercial world is also the speed of your moves and your expertise to foresee the future challenges. There is always a race to win over the competition and establish the brand of your success. The world is always keen to know the vehicle of your success to not only replicate the same but improve upon it win against you. Reaping the rewards of winning is itself a luxury as you showcase to the world the gamut of continuous running the race and winning over competition.

Speed keeps you in the game. Speed in this game of motor sports is never mistaken as rash driving but controlled moves within the given track. So, keep your game on in the given framework of your world and it will lead you to success.

We all are also being driven by our passions called Ferraris in our lives. Speed of success, owning luxuries and display of wealth all these factors sum up of our passion in commercial world. There may be someone "Monks who sold his Ferrari" but majority of us are running after Ferraris. We are driven by the desire of "Ferrari" or its attributes we may say.

In today's competitive world, the passions are to be fueled and on continuous basis. Running has to be made in given track. Vehicles of your commercial journey could be different but time limit is same for all. Risks are equal but your skills and maneuverability of challenges can bring different amount of success. Machines have learnt our behaviors and are acting as our replacements. The need for the hour is to build on our strengths like empathy, emotions, passions, "Ferrari" desires and sharpen our thinking skills to run the race with speed to add to our successes. Luxury and wealth will follow.

BALWINDER

XXIV

Friction- not a fiction

The popular term of assembly line functions is often found across industries where product development to delivery pass through different channels within the organization. It drags productivity and especially when it is found in interpersonal relations it also drags the morale. In one of the surveys, it has been found that 47% of the workforce feels that office politics or friction amongst the working groups is one of the top 10 factors causing stress at workplace.

Oleg Veishnepolsky, Global CTO Daily Mail Online says "Office politics are defined by self-interests and agendas that run ahead of business goals. Management is ready to sacrifice success to look good or to maintain control". It is a natural human psychology to pass on the blame when confronted in performance reviews.

Friction is real. Reason of it runs across working verticals from high aspirational performance targets, peer pressure, product success rate and leadership mandates. Culture becomes KRA oriented from individual point of view and very often Team/Organization focus is lost. Disengagement starts creeping in resulting disjointed groups having fragmented vision.

Feedback mechanism and rate of its implementation top down has an important bearing on reducing friction. Better shared vision through Objectives and Key Results for Team not individuals can also bring down the rate of friction. Last but not the least ego must be checked and never be allowed to supersede business results.

XXV

Heartificial empathy

The evolution of ways and means to remain competitively successful in the commercial world has turned human resource as a means as well end unto itself. Humans brought machines and then taught these machines to work like humans. Improvements were sought in human workings wherein decision making was subject of bias. Machines were made to learn human behaviors, patterns, intelligence, habits and languages to work effectively.

Now the need has been felt to add empathy to machine learnings and artificial intelligence to make the processes more human. Book titled Heartificial Empathy by Minter Dial asks for putting Heart into business and artificial intelligence. Reason that this key human trait drives compassion, care and cooperation. Empathy creates values internally with enhanced employee engagements and recognition of social needs.

One of the research findings say than there has been 40% drop in empathy in last 30 years. It is happening with a choice which is made in the name of survival. To leave an ethical world for the generations to come, Empathy is vital for humans as well as machines serving humans. It has been found that people working in empathetical organizations behave ethically in society.

Let's strive for Heartificial technologies.

XXVI

Human Resources-HMV

Changing times there has been a transformation in the ways of organizational working all over the world. Sales, marketing, manufacturing and delivery every wing has gone through IT entablements. The core component HR has also kept pace with adoption of modern techniques in its core functions. But all along the perception of HR being His Master's Voice has not changed much. It is still viewed as Policy Police and Boardroom insider. Any change to become transformation has to be adopted and implemented by all key resources. Human resource being emotionally driven needs much more than automated assessments and rule book directions to be transformed.

Present day automation/IT tools have already enabled the core functions being done by vendors like payroll management, screening of candidates. Even learning/ development has gone to open sources leaving only scheduling to be done in-house. This critical resource

"Humans" hinges on being engaged emotionally motivated and positively challenged with task assigned. HR seems to leave all these functions to vertical hierarchy.

HR today needs to take on the role of moderator, representative of its people's opinions and carry the feedback to boardroom for policy alignment. It needs to function as conscience keeper of a corporate. Work culture which often gets evolved on unwritten rules or practices needs to be kept in a required flow with HR acting as a guardian. It has to be custodian of such rules, policy and customs ever evolving with expectations of new joinees and experience of existing. To keep the working atmosphere positive, it needs to be guarded against rumors when perception of top-down communication is often opaque.

Be the guardian of resources not just gate keeper to watch on boarding and exits.

XXVII

Human Catalyst

Why do most changes remain exotic and do not reach transformation? One of the major reasons is lack of human catalysts. Human chemist Thomas Dreier explains human catalyst is where the essence of an executive job lies. Getting people with diverse skill sets on board in an organization is easy. The difficult part is ensuring that they work together smoothly. Since every bit of friction costs money, elimination of the friction serves the purpose of being catalyst to further the cause of change.

Ken Blanchard in The Seven Dynamics of Change said people can handle only so much change. Beyond a few changes, people become immobilized and may lose effectiveness. The workforce loses track and starts questioning what is in it for them. Catalyst addresses these concerns by channelizing the emotions towards progress. Management perspective remains around content of change whereas human perspective remains occupied with process as it impacts emotions, attitudes and values.

Since change is the only constant in today's world, to turn it as transformation, change makers need to be human catalyst. They need to understand the submerged piece of human nature that has values, attitudes, and anxiety over future. The change and its impact must be aligned with change maker's actions.

XXVIII

Intrinsic values

Learning never stops. It just needs open minds. Everyday gives an opportunity to pick the nuggets of knowledge. Pick the appropriate which enhances the value of your knowledge store house.

Sharing a new learning about intrinsic value system. Products or personalities carry and exhibit some intrinsic value system which drives them or defines them. Some products/persons are popularized through media and sales force/ influencers. Many a times some products/persons are made to do piggy ride on others and even put under arc lights for a push. These products/persons are advertised/ showcased by concerned corporate for customer attention, placing and or fetching market valuations. This process of selling, positioning or popularizing is evident all around.

Just think about products which stay in the market just on their own strength. They sustain selling/competitive cycle basis their core values. Net promoter score or customer recall value remains positive for them. But salesman shows it on asking not as an own initiative to sell. Reason is that this segment may not require regular push and may also not tick relevant incentive boxes for seller. Moreover, there is always an inclination to push for meaty margin products/processes.

Do not feel low or devalued if product or a person is not always on the showcase. Integrity, ethics, empathy and honest engagement with the purpose create shine that is never lost and also not require much showcasing or being put to backlighting. Shine of values comes out brilliantly on the face when product/person enjoys being in service and user/employer cherish the possession. Intrinsic Values ensure sustainable working and market life not the endorsements.

Be your own brand. Live by your intrinsic values.

XXIX

"Jo tum ko ho pasand"

"Jo tum ko ho pasand wahi baat karenge"………. are the lines from a famous Hindi film song still enjoyed by the listeners of all ages. The essence of "pasand" Liking, captures the thought process which helped in germinating the idea behind this article that is dwelled upon, while shuffling the pages of individual and professional relations. Caring about the liking of others is not just the monopoly of a hero/heroine wooing his/her love in a film sequence but it is the art which all of us possess and make use of very frequently depending upon the situation we are in. Deliberating on it a little further makes as aware that "Liking" is rather a nursery step in the school of relationships.

The other factor prompting to take on this subject again was caring about others' likes and dislikes. Often while travelling in a cab, the driver takes into account the identity (physical appearance) of a passenger and tries to behave accordingly. One compelling observation is the habit of some drivers to change the channels of FM radio/music being played in the car. During my travels in south India, often some of the drivers changed the channels to Hindi music as per their assessment of my likes without my uttering any word to change or throwing any sign of disliking at what was being played.

The above incident proves the point made in my earlier post "Surroundings" that you tend to behave as per your surroundings. Further the quoted behavior of such drivers makes me take note of the same and initiates my liking for such behaviors. This underlines one of the thoughts behind the subject of "Reciprocal liking".

Before giving a simple explanation to "Reciprocal Liking", let's have an expert view what the same holds in specialized field of Psychology. "This is a psychological term which describes the phenomenon of people tending to better like those people who like them." It further reflects the notion that we feel better about ourselves knowing that we are likable and enjoy the company of those who give us positive feelings. This also acts as a significant factor in the formation of our relations at individual and corporate levels.

Such liking leading to interpersonal attraction is a process which is totally different from our perceptions about physical attractiveness. It goes beyond being beautiful and attractive and rather takes into account the person as it is, and our acceptability towards them.

Why do we reciprocate the liking? The theory of Reciprocity explains that people tend to reward kind actions and punish the unkind ones. Moreover, we knowingly or unknowingly evaluate the kindness of an action not only by its consequences but also by the intention underlying this action. The rule of reciprocity further states that people help if they owe you for something you did in the past to advance their goals. It lays the fundamental rule that nurtures the habit of helping out other people.

The above rule of helping people and being a support in advancing their goals serves the basic tenets of "liking". The same is applicable across different facets of life being private individual or a colleague or a supervisor. It creates a positive impact in your surrounding when you know that your interests are cared for. Taking the same a little further, the implications of such "liking" can be more rewarding in organizations displaying the said behavior.

Liking is not to be confused with an urge of being accepted as it weakens the decision making in supervisors. Being accepted by all is not at all akin to liking. Liking emanates from respect also. You may respect a person out of compulsions or you can respect someone you don't like but liking is not under such compulsions. Respect is often taken as a positive influence on work engagement, relationships and productivity at workplaces.

Continuing further let's examine the ways with which we can have the positive impact of Liking at workplaces. This can be done by making workplaces likeable by employees. Let supervisors/managers be friendly but certainly not over-friendly. Show the team that you like them and are genuinely interested in them and their world. As HR scholars explain, the things that increase liking are similarity and praise. People tend to like when they find similarity of purpose, mission and needs. Praise; right from our childhood, it is ingrained in us that this simple trick works wonder.

As simply put by Robert Cialdini, Professor of Psychology and Marketing, liking emanates from host of factors like similarity, familiarity, praise, trust, halo effect, listening and last but not the least reciprocation. The reciprocation is the outcome of our seeking social approval and affirming our identities. Cialdini has identified Reciprocation and Likeability as powerful laws in his six principles of persuasion. In today's commercial world everyone agrees that persuasive skill is a predictor of success.

Liking also fails sometimes. It has a tendency to fail when attempts to be nice appear to be overly eager. Overfriendliness makes people uncomfortable and there arises a tendency to not to reciprocate.

Taking a cue from Reciprocal Liking, commercial world has transformed it into Reciprocal Marketing. Giving a space for your interests at my place (webpage) which indirectly leads to increased traffic at my space i.e., in internet business, is a classic example of the Reciprocal Liking in commercial sense. In the brick-and-mortar business world, reciprocal marketing is commonly known as co-op marketing, cross-promotion, or collaborative marketing or selling third party products.

As someone said, smiles beget smile, be it even beguile. Liking, with all true intentions also gets reciprocated.

XXX

Karma-the actions

A famous Hindi film song about love for the country goes like "Mera karma tu mera dharma tu". The actions and force or domain within which actions happen are aligned to the nation

.

At times it is seen that Karma that is our actions are failing to bring about the desired results as in charge of personal lives, family head, society leader or organizational leaders. The reason is that actions are not aligned with words. There is purely talk and talk but no walk the talk. When actions are seen as deviating to spoken words these appear hollow and lands flat on the thinking surface of the audience and fail to cause ripples in the thought process. Another reason is we as leaders of lives, families, society or organization tend to believe that our dharma is to direct and control karma of others. It causes major disorientation in the spirit of what your dharma is about - for the good/ betterment of all.

Catchy tag lines, mission statements, status lines appear cosmetic until the actions- Karma is aligned to overall good of the all - Dharma.

Actions must be made to speak in sync with words.

XXXI

Leadership nurseries

It's undeniably true that the main relationship wherein you feel glad on being beaten in pace of progress in life is a parent kid relationship. Each parent likes to see that their wards make prominent progress than the guardians. Comparably in history Guru Shishya custom was keeping up with similar spirit where instructor's name and notoriety was through the outcome of the disciples/students.

Coming to professional relationship we observe not very many such leaders or associations which can be known as nursery of future pioneers/leaders or the grounds-keepers of development. There is a feeling of uncertainty about their situation and power among the authorities. Team building or supporting ability stays restricted to how much transactional advantages being gathered. A well said Indian saying "Nothing develops under a banyan tree" summarizes the Leadership style of many corporate of the world. Liz

Wiseman an authority counselor calls these leaders as "Diminishers" affecting the viability and perceivability of individuals.

There are corporate like GE, P&G, Accenture, Unilever and Nestle to give some examples having kept a culture of cultivating the development. Individuals are tutored, sustained and permitted to develop past the shadow of pioneer/leader.

Key credits at nurseries of leaders are adaptability of jobs, getting rid of unbending nature of hierarchy of leadership for good thoughts, looking beyond personal successes, empowering workers to behave like leaders and letting light through to nurture the younger ones. Success of leader is estimated basis the number of future leaders prepared and permitted to sprout in the corporate nursery.

XXXII

Life of an executive

One of the studies by Mckinsey is titled "If we are all so busy, why isn't anything getting done?"

Looking across industries life of today's executive is somewhat like:

Clamoring calls

Fanatic follow up

Marathon meetings

Endless emergency

Waging a war

Micromanaged

Breathless budgets

Runs through a life

Calling professional race

Gains are monetary

Successes momentary

Filling up the coffers

Empty within

Shallow smiles don't light up face

Duty bound soldiers fight the race

Negating nature

Forgot the pause
Leaving the breathers
For whose cause
Corporate circuses make us play
Tricks of trade on human clay
Want a peace like smiling tots
Try being human not becoming the bots.

XXXIII

M L M...roles of management

Manager, Leader and Mentor are distinct management roles. These roles which are getting overlapped and generating a question as to why do we have more Managers, less Leaders and very few Mentors.

Vision, mission, targets and achievements are the words often found to describe the path to succeed. Do these words adequately measure the complete spectrum of success? Or can we restrict the 'success" in these words' description only? Does the success of an organization carry the same inference to its resources? The usage of words describing organizational vocabulary of success gets conveyed in different tones and shades from our Managers, Leaders and Mentors.

The shift in roles or dominating impact of other role defines the path of organizational success of resources. In one of the articles in HBS it has been emphasized that there is a need to look at developmental relationship as an underline in these roles. Most people manage for performance's sake rather than for development.

As defined in various management studies, Manager's role is cut out for meeting out targets and ensuring the achievement thereof. Meeting of deadlines, adhering to the standard processes and driving commitment to organization remains the "mission statement" of role. What drives the role effectively is meeting the numbers so that organization reaches the targets and makes a success. To nurture the career ambitions Manager's role tends to undermine the leadership and mentor responsibilities.

Leader who is tasked with identifying and creating new vision has to undertone the Manager within. Nurturing competence and ideation for new vision requires free flow of information and exchange of ideas. Opening up for accepting the questions on system, processes and management mantra makes the ground fertile for new leaders.

In the fast paced, target driven cut throat competitive scenarios in organizations, where and when do we look for or require leaders? It is not that need of being Leader is out of organizational globe; the role is more expected rather than delivered. People are expected to be leaders in their own situation whereas rarely it is found to be displayed by resources. That is the big reason why millennial is moving away from the need of "Leaders". Or resources are no more looking up to the "Leaders" in the same intensity as workforce of era of 80s, 90s or year 2000 used to look up to.

Mentors remind us of the earlier period of Guru Shishya tradition. It is not just part of mythological stories; it is much fancied by our millennial while they look up to their seniors for career growth or success. While looking for advice on developing leadership skills and overall development-Mentor is one role looked up to. The reason is quite clear as Mentor cares about his/her protégés by providing best possible support in providing chance to fulfill their career potential through teaching, coaching, and building high degree of confidence. A study by Deloitte on millennial found that having somebody to turn to for advice and help for developing their leadership skills was found beneficial.

The role of Mentor leads to sustained relationship and support which is critical to retain corporate knowledge and develop staff during their orientation and ongoing learning thus leading to success of resources.

Success of resource depends upon Mentors who are leaders within their own and lays ground for Vision, Mission and Goals for organization and resources. Managers are integral part but role in today's world has gone into silo as it has to reach the milestones and meet deadlines for quantified success.

Another important angle to Mentoring is who to mentor. In one of the studies published on mentoring by Delong and Vijayaraghavan, there is an urgent need to refocus on the question as to whom to mentor.

The success of an organization as found out in the study is on account of contribution made by majority of people bracketed in the "middle". Best and brightest may not require mentoring. Moreover, today's jargon of talent pool helps competition in looking at "readymade" resource being showcased by an organization that can be available to make a move anytime. Whereas the resource in the majority or in 2nd rung of ratings bring depth and stability to the organization they work for. It has also been found that they slowly but surely improve corporate performance and organizational culture of performance. However, the focus on only top rated, brings about a feeling of losing interest/faith by organization in this segment of resources.

The resource in this segment may never bring in the most of the revenues or on-board the highly sought-after clients, but chances of their putting the organization in difficult scenario is very low. With their continued support this segment becomes the backbone of the organization.

Millennial or workforce of today prefers to be mentored rather than just be lead. There is absolute necessity to bring out clearly that although Manager wants the job to be done, meet the deadlines and reach the milestones but interest in development of resources is also expected to be taken care by Mentor. Developing, acquiring and sharing/transfer of skills and knowledge are valued features of successful organization which when achieved through Mentoring leads to overall organizational growth which ensures the growth of its resources to complete the overall success.

Emphasizing the need to look after developmental needs of resources and need for Mentoring HBS Prof David A Thomas summarizes it as "I think all people want to grow. Not all people have the conditions around them that facilitate growth. There is something in people that's about change and development and evolving."

Manage, Leverage and Motivate (develop) the resources for a healthy and successful organization.

XXXIV

Modern Elder-New dimension in mid-life

We are living in the time of OLX and Quikr- modern day tool of selling the old and not in active use things for better.

These apps are much hyped to bring home the point of de-clutter of space/life for better productivity. However, the genesis has its deep roots in social system which made big inroads into our professional lives as well. Society per se has deep rooted reverence for the elders and this fact is well entrenched in our value system and upbringing. The same reverence is losing the shine in professional lives and in work places.

Let's take this journey of reverence to relevance and making of modern elder.

While going through a newspaper article on fighting various "isms" in professional arena one word caught the attention "Ageism" the term coined by Robert N. Butler. Like any other isms making strong impact on our social and professional lives, this Ageism is one which has made big inroads in modern professional lives at workplaces especially with the advent of private enterprises eclipsing the PSU era. This new ism is fast catching up with our workplaces as addiction to youth is fast increasing. This is posing challenge to not only the "elders" to continue to be counted among contributors but perceptional loss of growth by replacing them or reallocating the roles of elders to young. Our modern-day enterprise is running the battle with army of people attuned to pursue success at everything all the time with full obsession and continuous anxiety.

Ageing itself is natural progression and in every society elder command respect. Bowing before them or touching of their feet is a regular aspect of respect for elders. This cycle of ageing is for everyone and depending upon life cycle one endures it. Knowing fully well that ageing being natural process can never be reversed still demonstration of being young is first on the wish list. Nothing wrong in being young with spirits and displaying the same. Age in itself defines some roles and lays down the process of learning the ways of living while looking up to the elders. For the sake of old timers in family set up or in a locality there always used to be an elder doing the role of Google satisfying the curious questions of the people based on his/her experience of life. Even our folklores go gaga over the reverence for elders in nourishing the next generation with values.

Given the today's world every investment of time or money is immediately measured in terms of rate of return. Value addition or incremental cost of return is assigned to all verticals of professional lives. Any economist or student of economics will swear by law of diminishing returns. With the usage and time factor even, machines reach certain stage where returns or output starts lagging behind the output gained in initial years of set up. This will lead to up gradation and or process reengineering to align with organizational goals.

Ageism for human resource is one factor which may not be best fit in the treatment as done for non-human factors of any organization/industry. More so given the fact of increasing expected age of living and inflation Impacted living styles, ageism is becoming double edge sword for generations. Like our country having ever increasing eligible workforce in young is fast catching up the attention at workforce being open to putting in maniacal work hours with less cost. It speaks a lot about industry being opportunist and insensitive towards those who were there on contributors list.

Now comes the big paradox. Undoubtedly our society has a reverence for the elders. But at workplaces reverence is fast losing its place because organizations are run on commercial objectives. There is ever increasing infatuation for young across all industries be it advertising, manufacturing, IT, BFSI and even in politics. Within these industries there is again marked preference for "elders" in crisis. Even historically we see only the best and trusted men and horses were offered in the service of Kings. Perhaps decision makers today have a fetish to have army of "Yes Men" who simply believe in execution without asking How and Why of the decisions. Results are expected to be delivered "Any How" and in shortest possible timeframe. Sustenance is losing the stability. As rightly put by Psychiatrist Dr Sagar Mundada our workplace is fast becoming breeding ground of people blindly made to run to the end by any ruthless means.

Cost of contribution is the mantra. Bottom line impact matters much more than years of experience and wisdom. Often HR at workplaces silently starts ignoring or sidelining the elders in awarding roles or rewarding the employees. This approach fast catching up at work places has nothing against the young but highlights the fact of commercial objectives fast eclipsing the human face of organizations.

The need for modern elder is to establish the relevance at the workplaces. Reverence has to give place to relevance now. Richness and depth of experience need to be blended with youth energy. We need to have inter-generational collaboration at workplaces. Ageism is acting as denial of deserving rights to elders. As pointed by W. Andrew Achenbaum "The gift of extra years should afford time and opportunities to grow, to cherish bonds, to review life's meaning. Instead, older people often find themselves marginalized, which diminishes their capacities to contribute—and to matter".

The concept of ageism has been beautifully summed up in the words of Chip Conley. It lays down the importance of bringing out the need of creating intergenerational potluck at workplaces. It can help in people bringing what they know best and enrich the organizations with their contributions with dignity and staying relevant. In one of the works "Modern Elder" by Chip Conley it is said "What emerged is the secret to thriving as a mid-life worker: learning to marry wisdom and experience with curiosity, a beginner's mind, and a willingness to evolve, all hallmarks of the "Modern Elder."

Let the modern elder stay revered in the society and relevant at the workplaces.

XXXV

Nature's song

Dawn is inviting the sun to rise. Chirping birds and soothing winds are playing welcome music for the day to set up. With all efforts sun starts rising, expanding arms of rays in the sky. Sun travels through the day and discovers evening as an inviting friend extending solace of shadows. Tired from the day the sun slowly and sheepishly steps in and embraces the evening. Both spend some soothing time and transcend into the night.

Night, a great charmer, mesmerizes with her silky dreams and puts hyperactive life to sleep. Nature rejuvenates itself during this time and presents a fresh new inviting dawn again to bring another new day.

Such a sweet routine of nature is put as a luxurious dream for the urbanites who have engrossed themselves in commercial pursuits milking every second worth of its efforts in green bills.

Go auto mode, hi-tech, and even embed the technology to life but living the life must go a natural way. Changing nature's symphony of living life often leads to imbalance in resources vital for physical and mental well-being of the society.

XXXVI
Numbers Game

The numbers: an inseparable part of a human being. You may have disliked mathematics in your school or college days, but love it or hate it numbers are always there with you. Right from the first number, the date of birth to the dreaded numbers of academic scores and then the ever-expanding net of numbers be it cell number, house number, your beloved's number the list is never ending. The real challenge of numbers happens to be when you are the one who has to chase it or in management language achieve the targets.

These commercial numbers are also known as targets which without your permission travel to your dreams more so if you are finding it tough to achieve. But who has designed the theory of fixing targets the final numbers which remain close to the heart of all who matters in an organization. But why are these so sacrosanct?

All numbers do not frighten as seriously as the numbers which we call as targets. The transition of simple numbers to targets is seen as challenging assignment by those who have to achieve it and as fanning the hunger to achieve more by those who command such numbers.

But the question is can these numbers or targets can be viewed in isolation? What are the factors that drive the numbers to success, achievement or failure? Why does it appear to be so simple task when you are driving the others to achieve? And last what unfolds when saga starts to end with performance evaluation?

Performance management lays down the rules of performance evaluation. All these exercises are run on numbers. In an article on Performance management at Chartered Quality Institute, the same is explained as the art of management in achieving extraordinary results through the use of ordinary people. So, it leads to the game of numbers between humans i.e., one who are running behind the numbers and other who are running these numbers.

Performance management is not just running the numbers game. It is meant to get the results through the effective use of resources taking into account the environment in which the organization operates. The core area which requires the strategic attention while fixing the numbers is to simultaneously plan for the development of competence and capabilities of the workforce which has to run for these numbers. Numbers if are not commensurating with organizational capabilities will lead to stress all around and the scenario of under-performance will loom large.

Every responsible person of "Top Management" will like to put the numbers as aspirational but achievable. Simple reason for this is that nobody will like to have a graph which shows spikes or does not follow the rising trend. The need to create the environment that keeps your force motivated not only to reach your numbers but to excel is required as a prime factor for having a rising graph of achievements. It requires relationship management so that best can be achieved through the resources. Besides monitoring and reviewing the results at periodic intervals, corrective action whenever warranted to keep the competence and capabilities always tuned to the give the best needs to be in practice. This can come through training, workshops and ideas to have a relook on processes and the surroundings in which our resources operate.

Setting of numbers should be always looked into in the backdrop of designs and processes on which resources have to operate and deliver. Mere setting of aspirational figure without having willingness to change or fine-tune the processes to act as enabler for achieving the figures leads to conflict of ideas and result is under achievement.

We all may be having some obsession on numbers and believe in setting high standards. But to ensure that resources deliver on our aspirations, competence, capability, surroundings and motivation are the factors that require equal attention and review. Numbers alone may not ignite the fire to achieve but the surroundings, and combination of right set of processes can facilitate the burning of fire to achieve. Right kind of atmosphere is key to have synergy in the teams and which leads to proper bonding and gelling within the members for a motivational atmosphere.

The numbers game can be made challenging and a reason to arouse the sense of achievement if evaluation and rewards are taken care of equally well. Besides financial rewards psychological rewards also act as booster. Setting of goals should be realistic with an involvement of the team in having some say so that they can own the numbers. Ensuring that capabilities and competence do match the required needs through skilful leadership which not only manage resources but also empowers them with trust and authority to use as these are deemed fit in the use of processes to achieve the numbers.

Let's create the environment that our resources drive the numbers not the numbers drive our resources. Empower them to define the "Target" numbers rather than defining resources with numbers as achievers or under-achievers.

XXXVII
Professional learnings

Invest in your team and be transparent with them. Have faith in their capabilities and nurture them with motivation. They will always stand by you.

Smile on faces of your staff is a booster for progressive working. Give them space to open up and socialize within the teams. Occasionally ask for family well-being. Teams will learn too standby each other.

Continue to invent and invest in yourself to remain relevant in fast changing commercial world. Organizations measure return on investment in Human Resources at every stage. Carefully look at your runway of service left as mileage hungry organizations are always ready for dumping the perceived low mileage stock.

Ignite your passion and love for yourself. Keep some hobby alive to find yourself as a person before getting lost in hierarchical maze.

Learn to stay relevant and recognized for your capabilities. Evaluate yourself regularly. Whenever it is felt that you are a tool serving organizational purpose at the cost of losing out on your individual existence with decreasing relevance, take steps to pull the plug.

See to it that your loved ones are not served with subservient life. They do have a pari passu charge on you.

Update the follow up and follow up on updates is a killing cycle choking the bandwidth. Delegate with faith in resources.

XXXVIII

Proprietor and partners of progress: A view in corporate world.

Often, we find that while attributing the success in any organization/project first credit goes to proprietor of organization or project. The word Proprietor has been used to cover the importance, emphatic lines taken for execution and leading from the front, roles which are often seen to be taken by CEO, MD, Chairman or President in an organization. The next in the line of success contributors are those who execute the story of success i.e., the workforce. Customary credits are invariably given to workforce for building the company, standing behind it in rough and tough times and believing in the company.

On a comparison of the credits so attributed as above, it's the top person who gets the major limelight. Others are just covered on a swiping flash of light. Each CEO never fails to infuse this confidence that the contributors at the front line of execution in corporate plans are the partners in progress of the organization.

What's the compensation to partners in progress? First and foremost, they are expected to take pride in being part of the organization which is invaluable. Secondly their contribution in the company's success is enjoyed by all stakeholder's management, shareholders and "internal contributors- partners" almost in the same order. The rate of growth enjoyed at the top of the pyramid gets tapered when it reaches the bottom of pyramid. Organizations justify the same with risk and reward ratio. People at the whelm of affairs or management have a career reputation at stake whereas when compared to people down the hierarchy they have just one role at stake.

On compensation front, in a study published for US corporates, top US bosses earned 278 times more than their employees. Pay packet grew by more than 1000% since 1978. The gap between CEOs and median employees i.e., partner of progress is ever increasing. The fact is no different in other continents be it Asia or Europe. The pay ratio of the CEO and an average worker's salary in India was the second-highest in the world after the US, according to Bloomberg. The median remuneration of Indian employees was Rs 5,65,748 in FY17, while it is Rs 9.76 crore for Indian CEOs. This reveals a lot about the monetary evaluation of efforts of team called partners of progress.

Another angle to this professional story of progress achievers is our infatuation with role CEO. This class is looked up to as one of the networked, highly influential, very well qualified (Harvard/Oxford/IIMs) and born with silver spoon. The teams are expected to believe that CEOs are prophets or action heroes. As said by Subhranshu Singh, an author in advertising industry, "CEOs as a brand are priests who worship the high Gods of profitability, efficiency and effectiveness." These adjectives on the role of CEOs are not the only factors responsible for skewed pay variance. Higher the risk, higher is the reward. Our corporate top honchos do carry the risk on their shoulders and are often seen being branded as villains on account of failures. British Petroleum, Volkswagen, Wells Fargo, Satyam and Barclays's Libor saga are some of the sordid stories weighing heavily on reputation of their CEOs.

CEOs the "Proprietors" are like kings. They aren't elected to their position, they are appointed. Moreover, these proprietors are believed to possess unique skills to contribute to bottom line and top lines. Their leadership skills are not only impressive but scarce. They deserve high levels of compensation given their ability to withstand the enormous pressure they are under to create exceptional results for the organization. But without negating their contribution, partners' role is also not to be undermined. CEOs cannot run their companies alone. Other qualified people are needed to make it happen. Success of any organization is always a team effort.

There is a need for creative thinking on role and rewards for both proprietors and partners of corporate progress. There is no doubt about personality, charisma, positivity to drive the workforce and proven corporate track record of captains of the ship which they bring on the organizational table to drive its success. Although they offer their commitments for an agreed length of the time (3/5 years) as proprietors the partners are the ones who commit their lives. Loyalty might have lost its meaning in today's corporate dictionary of success but its contribution cannot be ignored. These are the individuals who keep the corporate steady and develop even when the economy/market trends undergo shifts.

Moreover, today's partners, the new gen of workforce look for tangible improvements and value additions to their careers which can give matching monetary rewards to have quality life. This generation is no longer a worshipper of proprietor role even though they are aspirant for the same.

In one of the studies by Michael Newell emphasizing the role of good management "Proprietors" in employee "Partners" development, it is said "Most critical functions of organization fall within two categories, value producers and enablers, with the latter directly generating revenue while increasing efficiency. Value enablers, such as leaders of support functions perform indispensable work that value producers rely on". To have a healthy workforce it is imperative to nurture them with freedom that allows flexibility and creativity to flow. Partners growth can definitely sustain the corporate growth.

Let there be reduced glorification of powers with role. There is a need for our proprietors to earn the reputation of being compassionate and ensure development that is sustainable. Partners of corporate progress are an integral part not just to be read in success stories told by proprietors to win them over. Their needs need to be acknowledged and rewarded on social, moral and economic platforms. Proprietors do need the partners even with all their managerial capabilities. Let the partners be encouraged to raise questions, dare to criticize and deserve risk reward balancing to establish healthy Proprietor and partner relationships in the corporate world.

"If you want to build a ship, don't drum up people together to collect wood and don't assign them task and

work, but rather teach them to long for the endless immensity of the sea" .... Saint Exupery.

XXXIX

Respect to Reputation-a journey through Trust

Any commercial organization is known for its branding or the brand recall value. It explains a lot about the standing of the corporate in the eyes of internal and external stakeholders and its contribution to the society and economic world. The world of advertising and marketing explains branding as an established reputation. Let's take the journey to reputation/brand building through stations of Respect and Trust.

For any successful organization there is no alternative to reputation which is essential to create the desired branding. Building of the brands is building of bridges between end consumers, organizational workforce, social and commercial space under the reach of business.

In one of the studies published on building brand reputation it emphasizes on earning the respect as a first step towards journey to reputation. The methodology of earning respect remains the same in personal lives as observed by human behavior experts and in professional lives/work places as found out by management experts.

In today's world where everywhere, there is race to add the friends rather than making the friends, the start of dialogue or interactions is always exchange of niceties, appreciation and acceptance. However, beyond the social media platform, earning of respect goes much beyond exchange of pleasantries as respect has to be on sustainable basis to establish the truth of your intentions.

Our messages, actions and behavior lead the way to earn respect. Same is the chronology for earning respect for any organization. Respect which is mutual and free from hierarchy driven obligations lays the foundation of building trust. Even though prime objective of commercial organization is profitability but no one could ever wish away the need to have respect and trust for organization.

Trust is the foundation of any relationship personal, professional or transactional and all kinds of social engagements. It allows to build the relationship that is expected to have mutual understanding, respect, faith and reciprocal concern for growth which can be personal, professional or at organizational levels.

Respect and Trust are the pillars which help any brand to stand in the market. Dynamics of today's commercial world is ever challenging the existence of organizations and their growth strategies but the one factor that encourages the organization to remain alive and kicking is reputation/ Brand.

In the words of His Holiness Dalai Lama "To earn trust, money and power aren't enough; you have to show some concern for others. You can't buy trust in the supermarket." The saying holds good more at workplaces wherein Trust establishes reputation for the employees and customers to mark the existence of the brand reputation.

An organization that aspires for earning respect to build reputation must have the trust as a foundation. Trust within the teams, with the communication, actions and display of organizational behavior. It helps teams, organizations and communities to grow on a sustainable basis. People/workforce tends to feel safe and develop sense of belonging.

Presence of Trust and reputation attract higher amount of loyalty from customers/workforce and best of the talent around. It also helps an organization to have higher perceived market value of its products and services. The faith of investors in growth story gets a boost in reputed and trusted brands. As per study by Reputation Institute (2016) around 40% of company's market performance can be attributed to non-financial factors associated with one factor called corporate reputation.

Trust also provides the common language to encourage honest conversation in the teams. It is the key ingredient to have openness in the system and culture of organization. According to Jack Gibb's theory of Group Development, when the level of trust increases, unhealthy dynamics begin to fall away, increasing the functionality of the group and creating a safe space for dialogue, debate, and problem-solving.

The said Jack Gibb's theory is centered on the TORI/TORRI model of pyramid structure. As can be observed the base of pyramid is **T-Trust**. Next layers are **O-openand**

effective communication followed by **R-Realization of common goals** and in the last **I-for interdependence**. Second **R-for Respect** has been addition to the theory which makes complete solution for ensuring group/teams/organizational development.

Absence of trust makes people physically present or participative but inwardly disengaged. Interestingly to make the teams talk about its absence again it requires some amount of trust to ensure that message will be understood in right spirits. The line of perceived increasing distance between individual growth lines and organizational growth lines appears on the corporate horizon.

One of the articles on Leadership Strategy by Dennis Jaffe calls upon organizations to check presence or absence of one of the key attributes in their work culture to find Trust is **"Openness and Vulnerability". It explains the important fact that a** leader who perceives he/she is "never wrong" never gets the truth from others. Dennis further observes that people are not quick to reinvest in a relationship where trust has been broken. They generally move on.

Loss of reputation hit the corporate financials hard when trust is compromised. There are live examples of direct hit on the market capitalization of corporate like Wells Fargo, BP, Volkswagen, Reliance (ADAG) and Gitanjali Gems on account of reputation loss.

If the desired goals are being a preferred choice of customer, earning an ability to charge for your distinguishing services, sustaining the support of all stakeholders then corporate has to go through the route of Respect, Trust and Reputation for building a brand.

Someone beautifully summed up the value of trust as "There is a possibility of hearing "Wrong number" from a familiar voice when trust is lost."

XL

Supplication @God

Lyrics of a beautiful ghazal by Jagjit Singh go something like this "manzil na de chirag na de honsla to de" requesting almighty "may not guide to destination, may not enlighten my path but give me courage".

These lines aptly describe mankind's helpless situation these days. Virus natural or borne out at greed of human labs is driving humans to nuts. Greed for money, success and winning over the nature is causing people to rethink ways to put mankind living in rational order. Development is good so long it is not detrimental to the interests of coming generations. Intelligence natural or artificial need not infringe upon basic human rights.

Time to look up to almighty to guide us to live in a more a natural way. Relearn the necessity of home, family, food, and shelter. Let us appreciate the value of free blessings of nature, air, and water.

Conserve the nature's blessings to leave behind a blessed habitat for coming generations. Need should prevail upon greed and let empathy be our lifeline. May God bless the mankind with courage to come out of the current crisis as a better, civilized, empathetic, and more rational human beings.

Supplication of a mankind.

XLI

Squid - Game of survival

Squid - Game of survival

Having garnered the world's attention, the Korean show Squid Game has generated discussion amongst all age groups on the plot of the show. Survival instinct among humans is the running thread of the story having patches of good deeds, greed for money and relationships revolving around one's own gain. It brings out the fact that man eats man world is a real one. Inequalities of the world drives people to go nuts and sacrifice anything but self for the pillage. If you find that the person ahead of you hinders your growth, get that person eliminated. Empathy gets beaten down heavily to survival. It is a survival of the smartest mind.

Nothing is achieved if you are not able to save yourself. Relationships, values, upbringing takes a backseat and get undermined by the circumstances you are in. Time is money and one needs to time the moves so well that their competitors are dislodged with a dagger of greed sharpened with selfishness.

Personal or professional lives, this show actually showcases the reality which we are all driven to live.

Squid the competition before it skids you

XLII

Stimuli of senses

"The complete man"
"Mark of a man"
"Scent of success "
"Woh perfume nahin lagata " he doesn't use perfume.
"King of the roads "
"A Diamond is forever "
"Because you are worth it."

All of us would have listened to these catchy, pleasing to ears and esteem awakening advertisement lines.

Ads play on emotions of fear, love, pleasure and vanity which are powerful drivers of consumer desires. These catchy words also tend to feed our hunger of esteem/pride.

Fear of losing on relationships or positions.
Love for being noticed and acknowledged.
Pleasure of achievement and celebration thereof.
Vanity appeals to sense of pride, importance and relevance.

All put together cause arousing of sensory nerves to action. Stimulate our senses to act impulsively. Slowly and repeatedly these words create a sense of desirability and our mind starts building actions as a means to adopt a persona.

Creative, cryptic and concise communication creates curiosity in mind to be the wannabes. Soft communication playing on our senses touching emotive nerves is an effective stimulus of senses prompting action in the targeted direction.

Just a thinking if such stimuli of senses can create a working environment at corporate world wherein achievements are not mere outcome of carrot and stick policies.

XLIII
Surroundings

In a corporate context, what would constitute the surroundings? From an individual perspective it would start from Team/colleagues to office space/design, supervisors, Management and corporate culture. Culture is difficult to be bracketed in strict definition but more or so it can be phrased as the DNA of organization. Information system whether is top down, or bottoms up. In one of the corporate studies, it has been established that feedback system that forms integral part of information system of an organization plays an important role in employee motivation. Giving feedback to staff and being open to feedback from staff creates healthy surroundings.

Clarity of communication with ease of understanding the message. Openness or the freedom to ask questions. Management reaction system towards the questions on policy or decision making. Nurturing of the talent and leveraging of the resources. Ability to take on crisis. Last but not the least demonstration of organizational vision & mission by management i.e., leading by example.

Off late many organizations have started investing heavily on creating the surroundings that radiates positivity and help in motivating the resources. Take for example office space of Google, Facebook, AOL, start- ups, IT and Data Analytic companies and MNCs. Besides creating a management process that invites participation with open atmosphere of questioning the processes and policies the infrastructure itself gives you sense of belonging. Role of supervisors adds lot to corporate surroundings. His or her capacity to take on changes/challenges with positive or negative approach can change the way team look up to new problems.

Dwelling on the similar subject, Professor Scott A. Snell, in the book, "Managing Human Resources," defines a positive environment in the workplace as an atmosphere of employee enthusiasm that improves organization performance. Workers reap social, health and personal benefits from a positive atmosphere. Organizations that fail to foster a positive environment for employees' risk hampering their ability to succeed. To have healthy organizations we need to have engaged workforce as studies have concluded that engaged workforce contribute approx. 20% more to productivity.

To have good citizens each nation strives to create the best of surroundings through society and infrastructure is built around the needs and challenges of the time. Similarly, to have good corporate citizens right from infrastructure to management culture/approach has to be built around the needs and challenges of time. The working population of today on an average is spending around 70-80% of their active life in offices/in working. The continuous interaction with colleagues, customers, supervisors, competitors and the world at large build a unique character around individual. The behavior displayed in corporate life also impacts our personal lives.

Happy and motivated workforce through positive surroundings can definitely contribute a lot in building a positive society. There is a need to have Gross Happiness Index based out of positive surroundings, besides having measures for profitability to know the health of an organization.

XLIV

The Dangal of corporate life

While most of the film stories are just made for entertainment of few hours and forgetting the same thereafter, few of them do leave a thought in your mind to explore its implications in our lives. Some of the thoughts are worth sharing.

First never let your aspirations or dreams die within you. Just keep them alive on the fire of conviction. No one gets the complete infrastructure done up for reaching the destination but some do look for roads less travelled. Means may be different or seem difficult but it is always the end result of your efforts that matters.

Patriotism, sense of compliance and discipline often crumbles when forced upon. Although it takes time to make it a habit or imbibe in your DNA but it never lets you down. In the opening of movie, due to Government diktat everyone stood after reading the message on screen asking everyone to stand up for National Anthem. At the time of climax national anthem in instrumental form is played for the winning country. Without any message or request by anyone, all the viewers stood up on their own as a mark of respect and rejoicing the moment of glory. The sense that prevailed in the end was far better than the first one.

Beliefs and practices borne out of experience cannot be negated in the face of modern mechanics. Like every match of "Dangal" opponent brings his/her own scheme of tactics to outshine the other player. Same way each situation in corporate life can never have a tailor made or robot answered solution.

XLV

The dying civility

"It has always been a mystery to me how men can feel themselves honored by the humiliation of their fellow beings," M.K. Gandhi. For the people who still recognize Gandhi and his contribution to social behavior will vouch that we are fast losing on his teachings.

Aggression, sneering, derisive laughing, ridiculing in public and to the extent use of expletives is becoming acceptable way of social, personal and organizational interactions. Look at popular shows like Roadies, Splits villa, Big brother, X factor etc. justifying the usage of high voltage and aggressive attitude.

Even in social platform the hate messages get more eyeballs than a piece from the saying of some sage. Just check the quality of interaction with a call center. People love to lose the temper in a fraction of a second because a set of generation has been brought up on the idea of two minutes Maggie world.

Personal or professional our interaction quality is getting murkier in a highly competitive world where winning is only way to survive. Ego kills empathy and Me first rules out all other options.

Niceties are now seen as weakness and killing attitude is a pre requisite for a recruit as if being shortlisted for a war. Commercial war is killing the social animal.
Are we heading towards hunter age leaving behind the title of a social animal?

XLVI

The Fault Lines

In simple terms fault line is explained in Cambridge as a problem that may not be obvious. It can cause something to fail. Geology defines fault as a planar fracture or discontinuity in a volume of rock across which there has been significant displacement because of rock-mass movement. As is widely known, energy release associated with movement on active faults is the cause of most earthquakes.

Moving away from geology, a famous book by former RBI Governor Dr Raghuram Rajan explains fault lines as hidden fractures still threatening the world economy. Fault is explained as a problem that may not be obvious or easily noticeable because of hidden fractures/inconsistencies in the nations' political and economic system. These faults prevail in availability and utilization of natural resources, income generation, poverty alleviation programmes, education and income distribution in the nations.

Another interesting word closely associated with fault lines and earthquakes is fissures. Human psychology terms it as a state of incompatibility or disagreement. So, connecting the dots on these terms, we find as to how we are impacted by the fault lines in our environment, personal life and professional world.

Fault lines are also experienced in personal relationships which appear on account of our incompatibility or disagreement. If we tend to repair the same with an open mind and cement it with faith in each other it is possible to build a strong foundation for life. But in majority of the cases there is a tendency to either ignore it or assume that it can heal itself with the passage of time. This causes continued anxiety, depleting faith and growing disagreement which becomes the fault line of relationships.

In many commercial organizations final product or service gets processed at different levels/stages. These level/stages are manned by workforce whose processes and goals are inter-related and inter-dependent. As observed by Dan Oestreich in Unfolding Leadership, wherever there is interdependency of people/groups which influences their work and relationships, there exist potential fault lines. Reasons are not difficult to find. People tend to be known as groups which get formed based on roles performed in a process of service/product delivery called verticals, rather than as individuals. Often one group carries the legacy of picking up the slack of another or correcting its mistakes thereby creating fault lines.

Fault lines also lead to silos in and around the working groups and there is tendency to perceive growing similarities between members of the group and increasing differences in perception between the sub groups. Studies reveal different attributes which are found to be related to age, color, sex, knowledge, experience etc. weighing heavily in emergence of the same. Fault lines often emerge under the continuous pressure of limited time and complex tasks of organizations. Reason is that groups are mentally attuned to focus on their respective part of processing.

The geological angle also observes the impact of internal/external factors leading to fractures and tremors across the surface. Fault lines at workplaces points out the factors causing such cracks in team performance and alignment to common goal. With the diversity in groups/sub-groups formed in organizations, the working culture plays an important role in creating a common thread of understanding. There lies an urgent need for leadership to understand the undefined culture that runs through the organization. Management experts say culture is like that part of the iceberg which remains under the water. It remains unwritten but prevails in all groups/sub-groups. So, fault lines require a deep study of culture that runs through organization to know the areas that require cementing or drilling down further.

As per a study published by Society for Industrial and Organizational Psychology, distress at workplaces caused by real or perceived injustice, anxiety and disengagement, lay the ground for fault lines. The perceived injustice is because of the decision-making processes at workplaces, perceived fairness in distribution of bonuses & pay rise, adequate and honest information flow and finally treatment of individuals with dignity and respect by supervisors. Since fault lines have been studied for their disruptive effects, this study also tried to find out positives from the same by suggesting formation of diverse/distinct work groups. The diversity on account of age, sex and experience can allow the group to be on the same page while discussing common organizational concerns.

Approach of leadership in managing the teams to get the desired results also determines the emergence of fault lines. One study observed that task-oriented leadership and relationship-oriented leadership both worked well in their own terms but have considerable degree of impact on fault lines. While one focuses on high level of performance with zero slippages and task takes precedence over relationship. The other type of leadership focuses on creating a culture of trust, empathy, cooperation between the teams, appreciations for individual and team efforts and thereby leading them to desired goals.

The workforce has an equally important role to play by being aware of the cracks/fissures that threaten to damage the surface of working together for a common goal. Appreciate, motivate and acknowledge co-workers within the teams on the basis of the contribution, knowledge sharing and help extended in creating healthy working atmosphere rather than falling in the trap of personality cult. Openness to cooperate and collaborate, sharing of best practices within the groups, evaluating the respective roles on value addition parameters can help in filling the cavities.

So be it a home, workplace, nation or world at large, a relationship comes into existence. Relationships between rocks as in geology, individuals as observed by behavior experts, teams as explained by management gurus, have to be acknowledged, given adequate space to grow, respected for contributions, appreciated for their efforts and recognized as equal partners of growth in respective life cycles. Realization and acceptance of fault lines in and around us can help in avoiding the dangers of the cracks/ fissures and help in creating unified teams.

As Simon Sinek said when people are financially invested, they want a return. When people are emotionally invested, they want to contribute.

XLVII

The Mileage obsession

The best example of our obsession with word mileage has been beautifully captured in the recent past advertisement campaign by Indian Car manufacturer Maruti. Its tag line "Kitna Deti Hai" (what's mileage) sums up all. Although it was meant to showcase the mileage strength of Maruti brand vehicles but it put forth the mind of Indian consumers. Leaving asides other features, the customer look into for making the decision, this "Kitna Deti Hai- mileage" factors weigh a lot in his mind. If you try to go beyond the reason, you can find the economics behind it. Vehicle buying decision weighs on safety, comfort, design, price tag and on the top of all efficiency which is better known as mileage. The last feature decides your running cost and to great extent the maintenance cost also.

The economics of mileage actually translates to our quest for finding the return on investment. Basic economics of every day decisions of our lives. Other factor that gets combined with mileage obsession is that it decides the life of association with vehicle. So, if you find the economics of the decision as positive there is a strong possibility of healthy or long relationship. Our economic orientation and human psyche on relationship does impact the decision making.

As we find in our personal journey and in professional interactions, most of the times mileage remains underlying our actions. In personal lives mileage is the possible benefit expected. Professional arena has mileage factor in every action. Right from the time of hiring, placement, career enhancements and allocation of key portfolios and selecting the key teams, decision makers look for the mileage. How the induction of particular individual or set of individuals is going to impact the top line/bottom line? What are maximum positives possible to be drawn out of the given workforce?

We all go throw the mileage expectations and many times review the teams down under through the same microscope. This fact explains the other truth of our love for numbers. Mileage is best measured in numbers. In any organizational set up, human is just a number. Your employment number, account number and productivity numbers ascribed to you for your professional journey in the organization. Any organization can quickly sum up the impact of an individual through simple stats called numbers. This is one of the basic realties that defines our work culture around industries. Leaving aside NGOs no one runs business for charity alone. Profitability and growth get factored in through the mileage measurements of the teams recruited to run the organization.

Driving the fad for numbers into leadership style we find that two different styles emerge. One style shows obsession for numbers and other which lays more emphasis on motivation, loyalty and performance. The former style of mileage obsession in Neuroscience is described as Task Positive Network of the brains. Herein the focus is always found on number driven objectives like profitability, shareholder value and surpassing the budgets to ensure the charts moving to north always. No doubt that number called mileage decides the rewards eligibility and lays the career path.

The other leadership style is explained by neuroscience due to the presence of Default Mode network in brains. This trait or activity of the brain lays down the attributes of attention to people, benevolence and inclusiveness which increases motivation, loyalty and performance of the workforce. This works as a booster to get the desired mileage whereas the first style basis everything on mileage.

The mileage impacted management science has found another model of leadership which is the convergence of management and neuroscience. Behavioral experts have found that better inter play between Task Positive and Default Mode of brain network leads to stronger traits in leadership styles which make good use of "Mileage" and relationships. Mindfulness and coaching help in developing strong and emotionally invested workforce. For leadership it reinforces the trait of better listening which helps in coming up with well informed and researched decisions.

Someone beautifully summed up the convergence of "Mileage" mindfulness and coaching impact with the saying:

"No toddler has ever said after they fall-down trying to learn to walk, this walking thing is not for me"

There is always a convergence of measuring how many steps in next attempt and encouraging coaching style of clap on every attempt.

So keep counting.............."Kitna deti hai".

XLVIII

The Great attrition

Are you being counted as a measure of achieving transactional targets? If yes, you are not alone as leading HR researchers across industries have found this harsh reality as one of the reasons behind the Great Attrition post pandemic. Change brings opportunities but also the realization of self-evaluation in core terms when you belong to a social group or an organizational team.

This pandemic brought about the fact of evaluation in terms of belongingness, being a valued resource at the workplace and being counted as a mere object of achieving transactional goals by organizations.

In one of the surveys, more than 40% of white-collar workers recorded contemplation to quit even without an offer in hand. No point in jumping to conclusions by employers that pay cheque or work-life balance are the triggers responsible for the exit because they're not always. A sense of belonging and being valued at the workplace is a major factor now. Relationship value is gaining more importance than transactional values.

Awakening on customer experience without learning of employee experience is proving a toothless tool to achieve the board room goals. Relational values, empathy and a sense of being counted in real terms as contributors can arrest the trend of great exit.

Commercial organizations around the world need to move away from cosmetic offerings and look beyond counting resources as mere transactional objects.

XLIX

The Sales Pitch...............

Pitches are like girlfriends so one needs to read them carefully to prepare a strategy to win the matches. The said saying by commentators for cricket matches lays a lot to debate on the Pitch...... be it a cricket pitch or sales pitch. In an opening session of any match there is often a lot of debate on ground, grounds man and one important person the curator. What might have gone through the mind of curator before he laid down the specific pitch. Too much grass, little grass or no grass. How it will behave with passage of time in a match and during different sessions of the game. How it will behave when there is a dew in the morning of late evening sessions. Bowling pitch, batting pitch or a dead pitch. So many words, phrases emphasizing the importance of 22 yards strip on which teams fight to show their strength.

Just carry this pitch to a commercial world and draw some comparisons with Sales Pitch. Across the industries, sales pitch makes a product success or a failure. Products across all lines like financial, industrial, commercial or other consumables all base their run of success on the pitch called sales pitch. Here again the players like end users don't call much of the shots. They are made to adapt to the pitch as is the case in cricket. Another factor the one who creates the pitch is directed by different set of factors which need to toe the line of producers. Like a cricketing body interested in public entertainment and making the moolahs, preference is often towards high scoring pitches which entertain the public better. Similar aspirations or interests direct the sales pitch for products to be sold.

Besides the genuine need products that are based on research of consumer needs and is adapted to the end user requirements the market is flooded with so many clones and me-too products that want their share of consumer's wallet. This scenario leads to laying of sales pitches with all kind of entertainment in mind without thinking about the treatment it is going to meet on game or product in the long run. Like the introduction of cheer leaders, these products are also clubbed with gifts, prizes, discounts and so many enticing offers to hook the customers. Since products are already there, the emphasis turns to sales pitch to hoodwink the end users in grabbing the eye balls and making the one called "sale".

The ever-evolving economy the over-crowding of the products in Financial and other Consumables market is making the fact clear that products are being made to be sold because these are there and not because a need of an end user has mandated the product. Rather needs are made to be felt. Commercialization has increased consumerism and sales pitch has played an important role. So, the role of pitch should be to enhance the utility and value of the game/product and evince enough interest of the players/ end users that they like to say "it's a gentlemen's game".

L

Transformation of HR-D to HR-M

Ever since liberalization of economy happened and numbers started ticking

in GDP, Industrial Production and Infra investments started happening, the

role of HR in industry has gone through a sea change. The perspective,

objective and role has been re-written in most of the industries like

manufacturing, trading and services. The major change factor has been the

service industry wherein financial institutions, Service Providers and IT

have remained the front runners. The opening up of economy has led to its

own challenges like joining of more players in the industry

specific area
and scope of extending services in off-shore centres.
Mergers, acquisitions
and take overs in India and abroad have brought new
challenges for HR.
Another important factor in transformation of HR
happened to be evolution of
IT and its impact on HR policies and management thereof.

The process of transformation that happened from HR role
as Developer to
Manager has taken shape in almost all industries at the
same or at some
variant times. Manual processes had a greater emphasis on
manpower being
the key source. With the introduction of mechanization,
and IT
intervention the manpower started being evaluated as cost
factor important
enough to make a difference in bottom line of any industry.
Per employee
evaluation factors like cost, productivity, profits etc. were
the new
benchmarks in evaluation of balance sheets. This
continued focus provided a
new thought process of HR being taken as cost centre. The
policies and
processes of HR started building around this new found
management mantra
of evaluating all segments on cost/profit basis. This led to
the beginning
of replacement of D (development) with more
encompassing role as M

management of HR. The Learned in HR science are moving step further

stressing that HR be better evaluated as profit Centre.

The recurring cost of wages/salaries being a major share of HR cost leaves

little room to maneuver. The flexible/variable part that moves on rising

curve is cost of investments made by HR in the workforce in the form of

Learning & Development. Right from selecting the right talent to grooming

as future leaders, this takes the major share of variable cost of HR and

weighs heavily in branding it as Cost Centre. The next reason could be

that this investment has its own break-even point. The benefits/returns

start accruing after a considerable period of time. These returns may not

match the timing of revenue streams of an organization/ industry. Timing of

investments and business cycle of organization/industry can definitely have

a bearing on the return on such investments.

The growing tendency of lean management and shuffle of manpower from

productivity angles, is adding to the concerns of how HR role should be

assessed as Developmental tool or Management tool, as a cost Centre or

profit Centre. Whatsoever be the organizational goal, this

shift in HR is
making it look like another organizational tool being
manipulated overtly
to get the maximum output through the minimum of
investments in it.

Human resource has woken up in many industries with
the slogans of work life balance, happy & healthy employee
and healthy balance sheet. Flexible work hours and family
gatherings also have made entry in to HR policies. But the
fact still is debated how to take the HR as cost Centre or
profit Centre or mix of both.

LI

Upgrade, upskill and uphold

Watched an advertisement on TV the other day upselling the upskilling as a reason to upgrade in the corporate world. One of the visuals showed a couple of workers just licking the unworthy (signifying pure flattery) to rise while another person is guiding the way to rise in the corporate world through upskilling.

It appears to be a rude but true reality of working culture that has somehow ingrained in white collar class. We can't just blame corporates alone for having such scenario's as working culture is equally developed/accepted/promoted by the employees.

Till the corporate working culture develops resistance to "yes boss" or licking ways to grow, upskilling or upgrading may not be of much help.

There is a need to empower the working class to upgrade/upskill and stand upright for legitimate claims in the corporate ladder. Real upgrade happens when "Yes boss" happily accepts "No boss".

Upgrade and upskill to uphold the values that ensure congenial work culture for growth of people with growth of an organization.

LII

Values truncation

Values are seedling of a character. These get ingrained in the person on every stage of life. We adopt, imbibe, fetch and assimilate values willingly and unwillingly. In today's competitive work culture, values are turning into mere book value rather than an impacting element in shaping behavior.

Ends are justifying means. Convenience is coming ahead of conviction. Silence is no more golden. Blow your trumpet so that you always get counted. Truth and transparency are used as medicines - as per acceptable levels of your conscience. Worries for the fruit are necessary to avoid wastage of your efforts. Know thy purpose. Loyalty fails to fetch royalty.

All spheres of life personal and professional are undergoing transformation. Inventions are few but destruction and reconstructions are many under the label of transformation. Humans are losing on empathy, meaningful engagement and cohesive relationships. We are expecting this behavior from machines.

Besides all these truncated value systems, positives are also emerging in valuing the present. People believe in making the best out of today. Money matters but its timing matters a lot. Respect and relevance keep resources mentally agile. Peace and mental health are getting valued more than flashy titles.

Change is inevitable but, in a hurry, to register transformation values are getting truncated.

LIII

Why the cookies crumble?

"C'est la vie," or "such is life," is a saying from the 18th century that originated in French. Cookies crumble if the dough isn't handled properly, or if the cookies are left out in the open to soak up moisture or are submerged in liquids.

Simply swap out the cookies for characters. If the dough of raising is not correctly prepared, it will be difficult to raise a responsible citizen. Leaving them out in the open is akin to putting them in non-conforming situations where dampness dents their uprightness. It's just part of life, and going with the flow is natural. Competitive and societal demands function like swimming through liquids, causing the cookie of character to crumble over time.

There's nothing wrong with standing tall or forming solid dough, but external demands, whether personal or professional, and succumbing to greed, take a toll on character cookies. To avoid moisture, you tend to find tight packaging, but that packaging becomes a way of life.

Volkswagen 2017, Boeing 2019-20, Well Fargo 2020, HSBC and GSK-2012, PNB in Nirav Modi, and Yes Bank are just a few examples of companies that have been indicted by industry regulators for having the cookies of character breaking in a rush to win the stock market battle or to beat the competition.

Cookies do crumble since that's life, but the conditions that cause them to crumble offer a lot to learn and make amends.

Take care of cookies around you for a better way of life.

LIV

You are being sold

Technology has transformed all integral functions of human lives. In a process we are also being sold. As a freebie to engage, humans are offered the stuff of their likings through push advertisements. Social media feed has started taking control of our thought process. Human brains have started processing the indirect commands being read out of media feed coming through our mobiles, mails and TV. Through IT and research analysis from Big Data, humans are being used as Lab Rabbits. Commercial world through Facebook, WhatsApp, Instagram, Mails, and TV is putting in programmed thoughts in human mind, which generate the results of their liking.

Impulsive shopping, tinkering with brain cells prompting action positive/negative and programming our choices/priorities all these are revenue generating sources for commercial world. We have been entangled in the web of IT/AI/Robotics/Data etc. We are being sold day in and day out to different buyers throughout the world market. We are prompted to take decisions on shopping, choices and even decide on affiliations to groups political and social. Human behaviors are being controlled, choices being filtered and decisions programmed.

Big Data is big Dad(a) of our lives and we can't escape this relationship. Virtual world is now new real. Watch it.

LV

Main Chup Rahungi (I will be silent)

There was a Hindi film by this name in early 60s. The name aptly described the silent force of humanity and its status in the society. The upbringing, customs and ego of a man always dictated and drafted the lifeline of women. With changed times and the opening of professional world for women there has been a noticeable assertion of Her rights.

A day commemorating as Women's Day is not enough to re-code the societal perceptions. Somewhere we need to bring gender neutrality in our homes. Kitchen corner is not a taboo anymore for boys neither is a corner office for girls in the professional world.

Let us now move to give what is her birth right. Right over her body and soul. No more exploitation of her body for commercial success. She has the right to say No both in a professional space and married space. Moreover, men need to accept that no means No and it does not have any other interpretation.

Let the boys also learn Main Chup Rahunga (I will be silent) wherever Her point of view matters.

Salute to Sheros of our world.

Slow Living- "babu ji dheere chalna.... zara sambhalna"

The biggest learning of year 2020 is if everything comes to a halt, life still goes on and opens new doors of learning the ways to live with gratitude.

Maggie mantra for living and expecting everything by a click is turning us into sprint runners. We run to win as if there is no tomorrow with a constant fear of being left behind.

A study comments on human beings as having become human doing. Always in for action or living with an urge to be in action. It is burning out the vigor in us very fast. Our age of rage is fast eating up our quality of living and we often seek refuge in wellness camps.

We are sacrificing wellbeing for achievements. Every earned penny or money's worth is not worthy if it does not bring peace or tranquility unto thyself.

Danish phenomenon of living known as hygge calls for creating a warm atmosphere and enjoying the good things in life with good people. It values quality of coziness, feeling of contentment associated with relaxation, indulgence and gratitude.

Slow and steady living is a win over thyself.

LVI
Perception narratives

Cognitive bias, perception narrative and attribution play an important role in information processing in the human mind. Despite all the technology advancement, these human traits are still responsible in influencing decisions about vital resource called humans.

Meritocracy, despite being fancied by HR experts, suffers body blow because these traits fail the genuine assessment or evaluation. The way augmented reality is changing the look and feel of the products on offer, augmented technology is required to make an objective assessment of resources which can be free of cognitive bias.

Let's measure all that matters to and adds value to organization and leave the matter that only measure up to one's perception narratives.

LVII

Work Place Aggression

Interactions between humans is a basic way of creating a sense of purpose and togetherness. Oppressive form of interaction becomes aggression which is intrinsic to humans. The good aggression is a reactive defense mechanism and bad aggression is said to be motivated by extrinsic rewards or achieving some objective at the cost of others' plight.

HR experts have often opined on the work culture and its direct correlation with health of an organization and its employees. The way individuals or teams interact gives a complete view of the culture of an organization. Ideals, mission and vision statements, catchy slogans etc. are all desired goalposts which need a healthy and positive form of interaction.

Aggressive interaction kills the interest to participate. Similarly, when teams are engineered to adopt aggression as a tool to get things done, it kills the spirit of belongingness and diminishes the urge to participate. Engineered aggression is a top-down phenomenon which teams use as a defense tool to justify slipups in performance.

Healthy work environment requires dignified work culture. Dignity is based on and established by respectful interactions within the teams and with the leaders. Depleting morale, losing the sense of participation and not being heard positively are signs when dignity is found getting lost in interactions.

Let's examine when needs of employment have shifted from food, cloth and shelter to dignity at workplace; does aggression in interactions benefit organizations?

A mental health concern...work place aggression is injurious to dignity.

LVIII

Wired

Technology has transformed all integral functions of human lives. In a process we are also being sold. As a freebie to engage, humans are offered the stuff of their liking through push advertisements. Social media feed has started taking control of our thoughts. We have started processing the indirect commands being read out of feed coming in our mobiles, mails and TV. IT and research analysis of Big Data are also using humans as Lab Rabbits programming behaviors. Commercial world through Facebook, WhatsApp, Instagram, Mails, and TV is putting in programmed thoughts in human mind, which generate the results of their liking.

Impulsive shopping, tinkering with brain cells prompting action positive/negative and programming our choices/priorities all these are revenue generating sources for commercial world. We have been entangled in the web of IT/AI/Robotics/Data etc. We are being sold day in and day out to different buyers throughout the world market. We are prompted to take decisions on shopping, choices and even decide on affiliations to groups political and social. Human behaviors are being controlled, choices being filtered and decisions programmed.

Big Data is big Dad(a) of our lives and we can't escape this relationship. Virtual world is now new real. Watch it.

LIX

White collar to blue collar

All around the world, whenever there are difficult business scenarios, corporates look for cost controls and look for pruning the same further. First sacrifice is always the staff costs. Easy to cut and control the noise because of prevailing employment market. Now looking at new found love of corporates for WFH and alluring cost savings on Admin expenses, next possible phase looks like of doing away with permanent workforce.

All white collar will be new blue collar working for specific project or job work only. Depending upon talent pool for job specific needs, people will be engaged. TaaS (Talent as a service) model is already making inroads in job market. Like floating tender bid for job and inviting interest for particular project.

You may get engaged with different corporates at different times. We shall have floating workforce not wedded to one. Corporates can cheer on no PF, gratuity, fixed office rental like costs and bargain for each specific job/project for lower wages.

Be ready with your quote.

LX

Zeal

The English alphabet Z is a wonderful creation signifying an end to a beginning which starts from A. The events, journeys, stories or initiatives whatsoever it may be called the whole life cycle of these terms is often covered with words A to Z of an instance/event. Every start A has to conclude for meaningful journey into a Z meaning completeness and paving the way to go for new beginning-A.

The word zeal in human behavior is driving force in initiating and/or completing the journeys of A to Z. It is the momentum that makes us to rise and chase the day and connect all the alphabets for a meaningful purpose. The purpose could be economical, philosophical, individual or team goal. Zeal is the real energy that gives us a push to make a move everyday and keep on moving despite whatsoever comes into our strides.

Finding zeal is like locating the source of energy that makes you to stand out as an individual pursuing what you are passionate about, what you love most and what keeps you happy doing despite all odds. Someone said that

Zeal makes you warrior and avoids becoming worrier. The quality of life is what your zeal drives you to.

Abraham Lincoln said "It is not the years in your life that count. It's the life in your years." So, zeal adds zing to the taste of life. Most of the times professional lives are driven with output/result-oriented strategies. It misses out living in the present or enjoying the process called journey. Riding on the train, taking the ticket and focusing on destination is travelling which miss out all that is passing through, enjoying the nature and living through the moments of travel.

Zeal, purpose, energy and alignment of purpose which keeps you mentally invested makes travel a journey worth living and retold as beautiful reminiscence. It does not require any endorsement, backing or external help as the trigger for Zeal is within oneself. As beautifully explained in the words of former US President Theodore Roosevelt, see what Zeal adds to the persona:

"It is not the critic who counts; not the man who points out how the strong man stumbles, or where the doer of deeds could have done them better. The credit belongs to the man who is actually in the arena, whose face is marred by dust and sweat and blood; who strives valiantly; who errs, who comes short again and again, who spends himself in a worthy cause; who at the best knows in the end the triumph of high achievement, and who at the worst, if he fails, at least fails while daring greatly, so that his place shall never be with those cold and timid souls who neither know victory nor defeat."

www.ingramcontent.com/pod-product-compliance
Lightning Source LLC
Chambersburg PA
CBHW051243130726

47988CB00001B/472